Who Created God

A Teacher's Guidebook for
Answering Children's Tough Questions about God

written and illustrated by

Michael J. Ruszala, M.A.

Vox Clamans Publications

A "proclaiming voice" under the patronage of St. John the Baptist

Vox Clamans Publications
Amherst, New York
www.voxclamans.com

First Publication, 2016
ISBN: 978-0-692-71309-9
Printed in the United States of America

Nihil obstat: Rev. Peter J. Drilling, Th.D., *Censor Liborum*

Imprimatur: † Most. Rev. Richard J. Malone, Th.D., Bishop of Buffalo

The *nihil obstat* and the *imprimatur* are official declarations, upon careful examination, that a book or pamphlet is free of doctrinal or moral error. No implication is contained therein that those who have granted the *nihil obstat* and *imprimatur* agree with the contents, opinions or statements expressed.

Cover art of St. Thomas Aquinas: 18th Century wood carving from the Philippines. Photo by Hiart in public domain.

Table of Contents

Abbreviations

CCC	*Catechism of the Catholic Church*
ERV	Holy Bible: *Easy-to-Read Version*
GDC	*General Directory for Catechesis*
NABRE	Holy Bible: *New American Bible Revised Edition*
ST	*Summa Theologica* by St. Thomas Aquinas
SCG	*Summa Contra Gentiles* by St. Thomas Aquinas

Michael J. Ruszala

Foreword

Children are quite the little philosophers. As a father of four, I know firsthand that they have an intuitive sense for justice even before they learn how to read. From a very early age, they question matters of fairness and equality. *Did I just see my bigger sister get a bigger cookie than I did? This cannot stand!*

Every experienced catechist has had that moment when an innocent hand goes up and a child asks a seemingly straight-forward question: If God made everything, who made him? How can we know God does exist? If God created everything, did he create evil too? Then we feel that deer-in-headlights look come over our face as we realize we aren't quite sure how to answer that question as an adult. Even though one of the most respectable tools in our catechist arsenal is to say "I don't know," it would be wonderful to be able to bring examples into the classroom to help students visualize some of the deepest questions of our faith tradition in ways that they can grasp. Doing so would invite them to reflect on and encounter the goodness of the Lord.

For this reason, my good friend Michael Ruszala has produced this much-needed book filled with examples for use in the catechism classroom to help befuddled catechists answer some of the more difficult philosophical questions that children come up with. That the lessons of the book are based on the teachings of St. Thomas Aquinas makes it all the more inviting. For St. Thomas, loving God sated his desire for studying about him, and studying God's mysteries increased his love for him.

I worked for seven years as a parish director of religious education before working full-time as an evangelist, continuing to provide consulting for the parish staff. During my time at the parish, I constantly trained our catechists to engage the intellect of the child so that they knew our faith was reasonable. Our faith does not require us to put aside what seems normal and logical. Indeed the attraction to the Catholic faith is that it is so reasonable. The Catholic faith sees philosophy as its natural foundation.

God, the Author and Creator of all that is, including the physical cosmos and natural reason, wants a relationship with us. St. Thomas is clear: God does not need us. Instead we are created out of love, through love, and for love. God calls us to a response of love, and Michael's practical examples in this book will make use of a child's natural sense of awe and wonder for God. It will draw the child to contemplate the truth, beauty, and goodness of God's creation and to reflect, through that creation, on the care the Creator has for us. When we draw children to use their minds to reflect on the truths of the faith, they are given the opportunity to respond by becoming disciples. That is the root of our work here in this book. If each truth is stated only as "fact" and not as an invitation for a response from the heart, then the treasures and examples found in the book will not have their full effect. To help bring out this effect, each chapter has a background for the catechist, presentation ideas for the classroom, and a meditation that offers that invitation to respond with a call to deeper trust in the Lord and abandonment to his providence.

Faith does not ask us to abandon reason, but the opposite; faith asks us to embrace what is most reasonable of all – faith in Jesus Christ for our salvation. I know you will enjoy this book as much as I did and if you are in a position to give this to the catechists in your parish or school I would encourage you to do so. I know my catechists will be getting a copy.

Adam Janke, MA (Catechetics)
Program Director, St. Paul Street Evangelization

Acknowledgments

One thing that is so unique about this book is that it crosses several areas that often have little to say to each other. Imagine – children and theological philosophy with modern catechetical and educational methods to mediate. This is the type of guidebook I would like to have in my own hands as I go into a classroom where students are hungry for deeper answers about God, and one I would very much like to share with other catechists who may not even be aware that serious answers to these questions do exist and can be introduced in an age appropriate way.

First, I would like to acknowledge the children and youth at the parish where I worked for several years as director of faith formation, who unknowingly inspired this book by their thoughtful questions in class and who kept the discussion going in search of the truth. I don't think I have ever taught an ongoing class in which at least some of these questions were not raised by young inquisitive minds.

Second, I would like to thank a number of individuals for their efforts in providing constructive criticisms and new insights which provided valuable contributions. To make this challenging project as effective as possible, I had sought out input from a variety people who have experience in the various fields relevant to this project to review sections of the book. Dr. James Harold, Ph.D., professor of philosophy at Franciscan University of Steubenville and author of *Introduction to the Love of Wisdom*, made these philosophical concepts come to life for me in class many years ago and provided further insight by reviewing sections of the book. Ellen Romano, M.Ed., who works as a special education teacher at Chestnut Hill Middle School in Liverpool, NY, provided a number of practical ideas from an educational perspective and provided valuable contributions. I would like to thank Adam Janke, M.A., the program director at St. Paul Street Evangelization and a former longtime parish director of religious education, for reviewing sections from the perspective of an experienced professional catechist familiar with these situations and questions. I also appreciate Patricia Marshall, M.A.P.M., a parish catechumenate coordinator and member of the Buffalo Diocesan Catechumenate Board, and Deacon Venatius Agbasiere, seminarian for the Diocese of Buffalo, for their encouragement and constructive criticisms. I appreciate Vince Vacarelli's efforts in reviewing a section of the book from his experience as a 20-year 6th grade catechist at my parish. Also, I would like to thank Carol Fontana, lifelong bibliophile and retired pharmacist who often wondered about these questions since her days in Catholic school, for looking over a portion of the book.

Finally, I would like to thank my parents, Frank and Susan Ruszala, for their encouragement and their many hours of proofreading, and also for encouraging and supporting me in the pursuit of wisdom through my education in philosophy, theology, and catechetics.

Introduction

The Reason for This Book

A catechist finishes teaching a well-prepared faith formation lesson to her class and believes she is done. Suddenly a hand goes up from a student with a very quizzical look on his face: "But who created God?" The catechist is taken aback. The catechist knows there is an answer, but she doesn't know off hand what it is. A trite one-sentence answer comes to mind to silence the student, and then she quickly moves on to more comfortable territory. The student looks down disappointed and then looks to another student. He did not get his answer, and he may never get a real answer. Given the way things are today, chances are the next time he will hear a plausible explanation to that question will be from a teacher in public school or in college – and the answer will be that "rational" people do not believe in God for precisely that reason. "There is no Creator," they will say, "just chance." It sounds intelligent to him, so perhaps he will conclude that this is the only rational answer and that what he had learned earlier about God is just myth.

But the student at the time just wanted to know. According to the ancient philosopher **Aristotle**, "All men by nature desire to know." Many adults have left behind their own desire to know. They have learned the hard way that society only values knowledge that is useful and productive. Knowledge of the nature of God has little practical use in a materialistic society where we just need to get by and get ahead. Yet the Christian tradition has always valued coming to a knowledge of the Truth and places considerable moral value on it. This is because Jesus is the Word of God, and all knowledge ultimately comes from the One who created all things. Monks, nuns, and scholars throughout history have dedicated their lives to the contemplation of Truth, and they believe this to be a life of great value. The ancient philosophers also dedicated themselves to the pursuit of knowledge about the most important truths in life concerning God, creation, and the soul. And as is often said, the child is the first philosopher. The child wants to know "why." Yet adults are more concerned with "how" and often insist on imposing that concern alone on children to the expense of the children's inner tendencies to learn the truth about "why." Children and youth learning about God have relentless questions about him – and this is a prime opportunity for engaging them and giving them a taste of the wonder and mystery of our faith.

Children and youth want to know "why," and the subject that is most concerned with the "why" of God and of life is philosophy, which literally means "love of wisdom." But modern philosophy has become quite a mess, from the Christian perspective, and many philosophers are hardly suitable to answer the types of questions that children and youth ask. The philosopher who stands out as perhaps the best guide for answering the questions that catechists are often confronted with is **St. Thomas Aquinas** (d. 1274), the patron saint of education. Like the children, St. Thomas loved to ask questions and find answers, believed unswervingly in God, and trusted in the reality of the world around us and our God-given ability to understand it. Many of the questions that puzzled St. Thomas are also the questions that puzzle children in class today. His approach was one of moving from the things of the senses to the things of the spirit – and that is precisely how children learn about God. Catechists know this well. That's why they have so many hands-on projects to help the children to learn about God – even more so in this age of smart phones and video games.

Most of St. Thomas' writings, though, are not developmentally appropriate for most children and youth. So in this book, I have tried to capture the spirit of St. Thomas' answers and package them in symbolic and bite-sized chunks for both catechists and students. This book takes eleven often child-like yet important questions which are raised frequently by students in class. I arranged them in a way that resembles the logic of how St. Thomas treated them in his *Summa Theologica*, which was likewise in a question-and-answer format. For each question, I have a brief section for the catechist for background understanding and personal reflection and then a section for presentation of ideas and a response of prayer from the class. All answers are grounded in the teachings of St. Thomas Aquinas, rethought in simple contemporary ways of thinking. Most answers are also grounded in Scripture, following St. Thomas' example.

In the chapters, each answer has a number of concrete activities which have symbolic value that catechists can use to help give the students some basic but real and profound insight into the Truth behind the questions that they ask. As symbols, they do not close the question but are meant to be seeds for further discovery into the Christian mystery later in life. Children will come away knowing that the Church has real and serious answers to their questions. There is a glossary in the back of the book to help catechists with any terms they may be unfamiliar, and there is also a brief appendix in the back introducing the life and teachings of St. Thomas Aquinas.

Faith Seeking Understanding

This book is not intended to be a textbook for class (since parishes and schools are typically required to teach by a particular set of curriculum standards) but a reference guide for 4th grade through 9th grade catechists in answering their students' questions. Parts could be easily adapted for use with other grade levels as well. The purpose of this book can also be thought of as partly apologetic – providing answers to difficulties about the faith. **Apologetics** serves **catechesis** by showing the reasonableness of the teachings. This book can also provide catechists with an opportunity to dive into these questions as well. Students should be encouraged to share their questions and their questions should be taken seriously. Even frivolous questions can be turned into a teaching moment, although the teacher should always maintain control – which often means postponing questions until a more appropriate time. Some catechists have anonymous question boxes, others have Q & A sessions. More often, those raw questions arise spontaneously when something in the lesson hits a nerve, and the students just want to know: "Who created God?" "Why did God create the world?" "What does God look like?" "What is Heaven like?"

It's often said that a mature faith is a questioning faith. But in encouraging questioning, I would like to make a distinction between skeptical questioning and the questioning of faith that seeks understanding. While both can be a starting point in the search for **truth**, it is the latter which drove St. Thomas and which I believe most suitably yields to growth in faith. It is a questioning that trusts in God who reveals and which reaches out for the **intelligibility** of what is known by faith. It frees one from fundamentalism by reaching out for the deeper reasons that lie behind faith. Students are well saturated with the skeptical mentality already since it is prized in our culture and society. Too often, being skeptical is associated with being intelligent, though much of today's skepticism lacks wisdom, or understanding. I believe in faith formation what we want to enkindle in our students is the wonder of a questioning faith that seeks understanding.

Why should this be held back from students? We shouldn't fear it! We should break down the deeper answers to their questions into their modes of learning. That is what this book sets out to inspire and enable catechists to do.

Michael J. Ruszala

Question 1: Does God Really Exist?

Background for the Catechist

Most students in faith formation, like most people in the history of the world, presuppose the existence of God, receiving this belief at a young age from their parents and others close to them. Naturally, some will begin to question their first simple faith in God's existence as they become more rational and critical. What students may not get, however, is that faith (our response in trust to what God reveals) and reason (the power of our human minds [see glossary: **intellect**]) are thoroughly compatible since both come from God. St. Thomas, who formulated the Five Ways to God's existence, likewise personally presupposed the existence of God as did the world he lived in. But he also insisted that this belief was a reasonable one – we can know its truth by observing God's effects in creation. For our students, St. Thomas and his Five Ways shows us that believing in God is just as reasonable as any truth students are learning in school.

A Reasonable Foundation

Students need a foundation so that they can stand even when some people they look up to don't believe in God or when they experience evil in the world that doesn't seem fair. They also need a foundation which will help them understand that God is not like Santa Claus or the Easter Bunny on one hand, nor is his existence threatened by evolution or the Big Bang theory on the other hand. As they grow into mature

> ### Helpful Tips
>
> *Don't get discouraged if you find this chapter difficult. Being the most fundamental chapter and reflecting some of St. Thomas' most fundamental principles about God, this may also be the most challenging one. While the ideas do build and understanding them is worth the investment, the chapters are written so they can each be understood separately as they come up.*
>
> *Also, look for the **glossary** in the back of the book to help in case you come across any unfamiliar terms. The terms in the glossary are introduced in the book in boldface.*

Christians, they should be challenged to offer a reason for their hope, understanding the reasonableness of their faith. St. Thomas, building on Aristotle, provides a philosophical worldview that is both compatible with science while also offering a deeper level of meaning than science can ever provide – a meaning that lies in God and is inexplicable without him.

St. Thomas is certainly not alone in the search for rational proofs for God's existence. In fact, the Church teaches, "God, the beginning and end of all things, can be known with certitude by the natural light of human reason from created things" (Vatican Council I, *Dei Filius*, no. 2). In 1802, William Paley wrote that as a watch gives evidence of a watchmaker, creation's design gives evidence of a Designer. More recently, C. S. Lewis wrote that God must exist because while there is something in this world to satisfy almost every desire we have, there is a restless desire for something that nothing in this world can satisfy.

The Path of Experience

Still rational proofs for God's existence are not the only ways to God but serve as preliminary and fundamental bridges from reason to faith which some people find helpful. For a student who is seriously struggling with God's existence nowadays, oftentimes the best approach is first sharing our experience of God through personal witness. There are often other issues young people are dealing with and they need to feel accepted by the faith community and see God's love and action here and now. Incorporating on-topic witness stories into the catechetical lesson can be an effective way of bringing the faith to life for the students, enabling them to experience the life of faith through you and also yielding more credibility in their eyes to what you have to say. A personal witness need not be on anything extraordinary such as a miracle or radical conversion – though these can certainly be quite powerful. Any sincere moment of grace will do. Perhaps start by setting up your experience of needing God's grace, telling how you believed God's grace intervened, and relating it to your spiritual journey with Christ in the Church.

St. Thomas' Five Ways for God's Existence (ST I, 2, 3)

The Five Ways were important to St. Thomas since he placed them towards the beginning of his *Summa Theologica*. They provide many of the principles needed for his discussion on the nature of God. These principles are very relevant to us because many of the keys to answering students' questions lie here. All the Five Ways, drawing from the effects of God in creation, tell of various unique attributes of God or relationships to the world. Below I will draw a very basic sketch of these Five Ways. It may not be necessary to go over each of the Five Ways in your class – you can be selective and effectively make the point.

1. Motion

St. Thomas' First Way considers the motion of all the things in the world and traces it back to God who is ultimately responsible for setting the world in motion in the first place.

In our world, we see moving things – people, animals, clouds, wheels, etc. Every moving thing was ultimately moved by another. For example, clouds are moved by air, air is moved when it changes temperature, which has to do with the vibration of molecules, which is caused by other forces, etc. Nothing is the ultimate mover of itself. Yes, we move our arms and legs, but it certainly wasn't us who put ourselves in motion in our mother's womb! If there were no first mover which did not itself need to be put in motion, nothing else would move. And this first mover, or Unmoved Mover, everyone calls God.

Further the only thing that often gets us up on an early morning is our free will – choosing to be on time for work rather than staying nestled under the covers. But even our free will needed an ultimate mover. God created our free will and, being the ultimate Good, made **goodness** attractive to it. And he provided a world of good things for it to be attracted to. For example, after a moving speech, people often say they are "moved" to action. Ultimately they are moved by their perception of goodness on loan from God, even if their choice is for a lesser good than God intended for them (see Question 7: "If God Created Everything, Did He Create Evil?").

2. The Coming-To-Be of Things (efficient cause)

St. Thomas' Second Way considers how everything comes into being from something else, which in turn came into being from something else – and the one who started this chain must be God the Creator.

It is helpful to note that an "efficient cause" is Aristotle's term for something that brings something else into the type of **being** it is. For example, the sculptor made the statue what it is. But certainly the sculptor didn't bring the marble into being. It was formed by pressures and forces in the earth for long periods of time. And before that, the material was a different form of mineral.

Or if the Big Bang theory is true, Earth goes back to a single cosmic energy concentration which spiraled out into a multitude of stars and planets whose forces were constantly operating, forming various minerals, gasses, etc. But this doesn't explain what brought the substance behind the "Big Bang" into being, since it is just a being potentially among other beings with nothing necessary about it. For the things that exist now to exist, there must be a cause that first brings all beings into existence – and the "Big Bang" doesn't have the type of attributes needed. (For more on the Big Bang theory, see the background for Question 3: "Who Created God?")

The First Cause, prior to a "Big Bang" or anything else, is what we call God.

3. A Necessary Being (possibility and necessity)

In his Third Way, St. Thomas considers how all the things that are capable of coming into and out of being depend on one Being which is absolutely permanent and immune from coming into and out of being – and this is God.

Everything in our direct experience – people, animals, plants, clouds, etc. – came into existence at some point, which means that at one point they did not exist. But if all the beings of this sort at some point did not exist, then even now, nothing would exist. So there must be a being of a different sort – a **Necessary Being**, who simply is. But any being that can be destroyed cannot be the Necessary Being, because then it would go out of existence. God told Moses in Exodus 3:14, "I am who I am." He is the Necessary Being. (For more on God as the Necessary Being, see Question 3: "Who Created God?")

4. A Most Perfect Being (gradation)

In his Fourth Way, St. Thomas considers how things that are perfect in some ways must reflect something that is perfect in all ways – and this is God.

Our notions of goodness, truth, and beauty (see glossary: **transcendentals**) must have a standard that they are based on, and this standard must be in all ways good, true, and beautiful. In other words, all beings in our experience reflect this standard to one extent or another. This standard, and this most noble Being, is God. (See Question #11: "If Something is Wrong in One Culture, Could it Be Right in Another Culture?" for more on this standard.)

5. The Order and Goal of Things (**teleology**)

In his Fifth Way, St. Thomas considers how all things in the world have purpose and how this must have been given them by God who is their ultimate end.

All beings have meaning or direction. Even those beings which lack the intelligence to choose their ends somehow act for those ends. For example, animals of any given species act in a consistent way because of their instincts, which guide them towards their survival. Birds build nests and fly south for the winter. But this purpose must have been implanted in them by an Intelligence. This we call God, who created and ordered all things. Further, the ultimate purpose (see glossary: **final end**) of all creatures is to give **glory** to God by reflecting his excellence in some small way.

Even in the theory of **evolution**, the biological movement of evolution is directed towards something as an end. This end is survival. The claws of the tiger are said to have evolved to enable the tiger to feed itself, the fins of a fish to propel the fish underwater, and the instinct of birds to build nests to keep their young warm. A healthy animal whose species survives through the eons is a reflection of God's glory. For **humans**, the reflection of God's glory does not stop at survival but at the full thriving of body and **soul** which is not complete until we are given the gift of seeing God in Heaven (see Question 4: "What Does God Look Like?"). In fact, for humans, survival is even worth sacrificing in order to attain Heaven.

Reflection for the Catechist

o Why did you first believe in God? Why do you believe in God now?

o Where do you experience God in your life? Was there a moment or process that awakened you to it?

o Why are faith and reason compatible? Why do many people today not believe that they are?

o Which of the Five Ways do you gravitate to the most, and why?

o Consider the way in which St. Thomas approaches God in the Five Ways. What is common to each of the ways?

o What purpose could the Five Ways serve in one's life of faith?

Presentation Ideas

Key Concept: Even before faith, we can know God's existence by looking at what he has made (creation).

Scripture: "There are things about God that people cannot see – his eternal power and all that makes him God. But since the beginning of the world, those things have been easy for people to understand. They are made clear in what God has made." – Romans 1:20 (ERV)

Activities

• **Witness Story:** Share a moment you knew for yourself that God is real. Share what it was like beforehand, how God intervened, and how it affected your walk with Christ within the Church.

1st Way: Motion

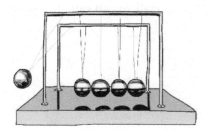

Activity: Set up a Newton's Cradle Pendulum. Otherwise show a picture or search for an online video clip of one.

Symbols: The pendulum represents the world and everything that is moving now. The person who sets the pendulum in motion represents God.

Explanation: Explanation: Nothing ultimately moves itself but is moved by something else. It takes something not part of the pendulum to start it moving. A person pulls back one of the balls and lets it swing, starting a repeated reaction. In a similar way, the moving things in our world needed a first unmoved Mover. Please note that God created everything from nothing, but right now, we're just talking about the movement of things. Draw from and discuss St. Thomas' 1st Way.

2nd Way: The Coming-To-Be of Things

Activity: Draw a diagram like the one pictured below on the blackboard, or photocopy this one. Split the students into groups to draw diagrams to trace as far back as they can image where certain things came from. Assign one thing for each group to trace back its causes: an apple, a student from the class, a pencil, a flower, a dog, a table, etc.

Chain of Causes

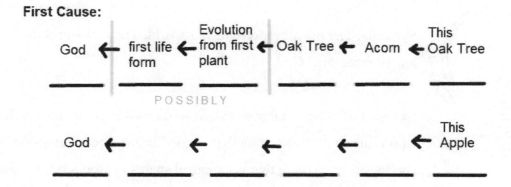

Explanation: God always has to come first in the chain, or else the chain will have no real beginning. If the furthest the students can trace the thing is still only to another created being, show how that doesn't go far enough back. If there were no first cause to bring all beings into existence, nothing in our world would exist. Draw from and discuss St. Thomas' 2nd Way.

3rd Way: A Necessary Being

Activity: Point to a table and ask students to think of ways the table could get destroyed. The table could get burned, chopped up, broken, etc. Then ask the students about mountains – can they be destroyed? Yes. I.e. Earthquakes, erosion, etc. Tell the students that God isn't like that at all. He is indestructible.

Symbols: The table represents anything that has parts and can get broken up. This is contrasted with God, who does not need parts and cannot be injured or harmed because he simply *is*.

Explanation: Any thing that can stop existing cannot be ultimately responsible for the existence of the world. If all the beings that don't have to exist didn't exist, there would be no beings now. There must be a Necessary Being, who simply is – always and forever. As God revealed his Name in Exodus 3:14, "I am who I am." Draw from and discuss St. Thomas' 3rd Way. (For more, see Question 3: "Who Created God?")

4th Way: A Most Perfect Being

Activity: Pass around a small mirror and have the students look into it.

Symbols: The mirror represents our world. The real world that's reflected by the mirror represents God.

Explanation: We and our world, in so far as it is good, are a reflection of God, who is all good. Everything that is good is good because it shares in God's goodness. Everything that is beautiful shares in God's beauty. Ask how we know that love is good and hate is bad. Because we all have a standard in our hearts which comes from God. Draw from and discuss St. Thomas' 4th Way.

5th Way: The Order and Purpose of All Things

Activity: Ask students to describe something they have made or built. Ask them what purpose it has. i.e. If a boy whittled a walking stick, it's to help with hiking. What types of things do dogs or cats do by instinct? i.e. bark, chase, run from danger, etc. Those are ways their Creator designed them for a purpose. Talk about different parts of animals: wings, claws, duck bills, etc. What purposes do they serve? They help the animal survive. Ultimately the animal's existence gives glory to God.

Explanation: As we make things for a purpose, we can see purpose within creation. The ultimate purpose or end of all things is God. This too is an evidence of an intelligent Creator. This also means that God created each and every one of us with a purpose in mind.

Further: Even in the theory of evolution, the end is survival, and the survival of a species gives glory to God. Draw from and discuss St. Thomas' 5th Way. (See Question 9: "Aren't Humans Just Monkeys with Bigger Brains?" for more on evolution.)

Review

After completing selected activities, have the students pair up and basically explain to each other one of the Five Ways for God's Existence.

9

Prayer Service: Praise of the Lord of Creation

Leader: In the Name of the Father, and of the Son, and of the Holy Spirit.

All: Amen.

Reader 1: Before the world began, the Word was with God, and the Word was God. He was with God in the beginning... Everything was made through him and nothing was made without him (Jn. 1:1-3 [ERV]).

Leader: We praise you Lord God, Creator of All! You speak and your word is done. All creation reveals your glory.

Side 1: The heavens tell about the glory of God.

Side 2: The skies announce what his hands have made.

Side 1: Each new day tells more of the story.

Side 2: And each night reveals more and more about God's power (Ps. 19:1-2 [ERV]).

Reader 2: Lord, you created so many things! With your wisdom you made them all. The earth is full of the living things you made.

Reader 1: Lord, all living creatures depend on you. You give them food at the right time. You give it, and they eat it. They are filled with good food from your open hands.

Reader 2: When you send out your life-giving spirit, things come alive, and the world is like new again! (Ps. 104:24, 27, 30 [ERV]).

Leader: You, O Lord, are Goodness, Truth, and Beauty itself. Everything we have is a gift from you.

Side 1: Praise the Lord, you heavenly angels! Praise the Lord's glory and power.

Side 2: Praise the Lord and honor his name! Worship the Lord in all his holy beauty!

Side 1: The Lord ruled as king at the time of the flood, and the Lord will rule as king forever.

Side 2: May the Lord make his people strong. May the Lord bless his people with peace (Ps. 29:1-2, 10-11 [ERV]).

Leader: Glory be to the Father, and to the Son, and to the Holy Spirit.

All: As it was in the beginning, is now, and ever shall be, world without end. Amen.

Question 2: Why Did God Create the World? Was He Lonely?

Background for the Catechist

It takes either a child or a philosopher to wonder at something so removed from the work-a-day world of practical choices and responsibilities. The act of wondering is something so utterly human – just try to imagine even the "smartest" animal pondering it. According to Socrates, "Wonder is the beginning of wisdom." So let's take the students beyond curiosity to that wonder which is so close. Something awesome lies behind this simple question – the nature of God.

To understand "why," first we have to understand "what." St. Thomas took as a principle that a being acts as it is. He would examine the "nature" of a being, determining its powers. What is God like? By human reason, we can know what God *isn't* by taking away every imperfection – and that includes being lonely (ST 1, 3). By faith we can peer a bit further into what God is like by what he revealed in Scripture and Tradition – and there he revealed that he is a **Trinity** of Persons. Now let's take a closer look at this.

God's Blessedness: No Room for Loneliness

God lacks nothing; he is most happy, or blessed. We, on the other hand, can be lonely because we have a need for friendship which is sometimes not met. According to St. Thomas, happiness consists in exercising one's powers to the fullest on their proper object (SCG 1.100). For example, people say they feel fulfilled when they are using their gifts, talents, and capacity for **love** to their full potential. God is Spirit, and the powers of **spirit** are to know and to love. From all eternity, God knows and loves himself – after all, God is the noblest being to know and love (SCG 1.102). God's infinite love and knowledge of himself is utterly fulfilling – after all, what better object of knowledge and love could there possibly be? And in light of our Christian belief in the Trinity, it makes even more sense that God is not lonely.

11

God: A Loving Community of Persons

In the Gospels, Jesus revealed three relations in the one God – Father, Son, and Holy Spirit. By his words and actions, Jesus revealed that he himself is divine. He also prayed to God his Father, with whom he had an incredibly intimate relationship. Jesus further said that he and his Father will send us a Spirit, whose attributes are also divine. These three equal Persons of the Trinity existed in relation from all eternity. According to St. Thomas, the Father is the Origin, the Son is the Image or Word which proceeds from the Father, and the Holy Spirit is the Love proceeding from the Father and the Son (ST I, 34, 1; ST I, 37, 1). God is three Persons – not three "people" walking around, but three infinite relations so intense that each can say "I." While the Trinity is a mystery, its result makes perfect sense: God infinitely knows and loves himself from all eternity and is never lonely. This is what we mean when with St. John we say that God is Love.

Creation: The Free Outpouring of God's Goodness

So if God didn't need the world to be happy, why then did he create it? St. Thomas taught that God, being infinitely good, freely chose to create the world so that he could share his goodness with creatures (SCG 1.81). Following in the philosophical tradition of Plato, goodness seeks to communicate itself. It is like a couple getting married who desires to share their joy by inviting many friends and family to the service and the feast. In this line of the sharing of goodness, St. Thomas quotes St. Augustine who taught, "Because God is good, we exist" (SCG 2.28). What a wonderful reason for existing! What an awesome truth to share with a child.

God's outpouring of goodness is reflected in the diversity of creation (ST I, 47, 1). No one being could express the full goodness of God, and even the whole of creation is but an **analogy** of its Creator. The world is placed beneath the rule of rational creatures, which are the crown of God's creation. But it doesn't stop there. It goes back to the Trinity. God brought us rational creatures into being not only to share his goodness by existing as we do, but also so that we could become his own children. A child shares his parent's nature. St. Paul tells us that as Christians and thus children of God, we share the divine nature! This means the Trinity dwells in our souls and makes us more pleasing to God.

The Meaning of Life

Many people remember the answer of the *Baltimore Catechism* to the question "Why did God make you?" "God made me to know Him, to love Him, and to serve Him in this world, and to be happy with Him forever in the next" (I, I, 6). This is quite true and can stay forever with the children who learn it. Just like God the Trinity knows and loves himself, so we, as rational creatures, are called to know and love him as sons and daughters, and to serve him in all we do. This is why God created the world – for the sake of rational creatures who are called to know, love, and serve him.

Reflection for the Catechist

- o   Why is it that before we answer the question "Why did God create the world" we have to ask what God is like? (See second paragraph.)
- o   Do you agree that if God is most blessed then he could never really be lonely? Why or why not?
- o   Recall a joyful moment in your life when you felt the desire to share your joy with others. What was that like, and what does it tell us about God and creation?
- o   What difference do you think it makes in our faith that we believe God is Trinity – a community of love? What does that say about how Christians see God's creation and his care for us?
- o   Have you ever wondered about the meaning of life or felt that you weren't sure about its meaning? What is it like not to know the meaning of life – whether or not one is conscious of the need for it? How does our Christian faith awaken us to our need for meaning and direct us in our search for it?

Presentation Ideas

Key concept: God – Father, Son, and Spirit – is most happy and never lonely because God knows and loves himself. God created the world to share his goodness, which is seen in all creation. God's goodness is seen above all in his call for us to know, love, and serve him as his own children.

Saint quote: "Because God is good, we exist." – St. Augustine

God Cannot Be Lonely

Activity #1: Make the sign of the cross with the students.

Symbol: The sign of the cross represents the Trinity.

Explanation: Point out that this is an expression of our belief that from all eternity, God is three Persons but one God. This is because of what Jesus taught us about God in the Gospels. The Bible tells us that God is Love – he is a community of persons in total and inseparable love. God could never be lonely. With the Trinity, it is like spending time with really amazing friends.

15th century Russian icon The Trinity *by Andrei Rublev (public domain)*

Connection: Have the students name some qualities they look for in a good friend. God is the best friend imaginable. He is the Source of all good things. Each Person of the Trinity shares this amazing friendship. They invite us into this as well!

Activity #2: Show an icon representing the Trinity. Then have the students draw their own creative representation of God as Trinity with love and self-knowledge.

Explanation: Icons are "written" as a prayer and all the figures, positions, and colors have meaning – even though the image may not be lifelike as a photograph would be.

God Freely Chose to Share His Goodness

Activity: Bring in pictures of a wedding and ask how many students have ever been to one. Say an older sister or cousin is getting married and is very happy. Ask the students: who would she invite to the wedding? She *could* just have a private wedding: only the bride, the groom, the priest, and two witnesses – and she'd still be married and could be very happy with her husband. But how would it make her feel to share her special day with many friends and family?

Symbols: The happy couple who wants to share their joy represents God who wants to share his joy with creation – and especially people.

Explanation: God could have been happy without creation since he knows and loves himself from all eternity. But he wanted to share his great goodness with us. Because God is good, we exist!

Chart: All Creation Shares in God's Goodness

Explanation: Everything good is from God but expresses him in different ways.

	Rocks	Plants	Animals	Humans
Spirit				✓
Senses			✓	✓
Life		✓	✓	✓
Being	✓	✓	✓	✓

We Are Created to Know, Love, and Serve God

Proclaim: Teach students the three reasons for which God created us – to know him, to love him, and to serve him.

Activity: Have the students make a "foldable" organizer, as shown in the picture. On the outer fold, have the students write, "Know Him," "Love Him," and "Serve Him," and on the inner part that corresponds to each concept, have them write examples or draw pictures of each.

Explanation: That we are created to know, love, and serve God means that we need to be in a relationship with him in order to be truly happy and fulfilled.

Review

Have students pair up to give an answer to the question "why did God create the world?" and "was he lonely?"

Prayer Service: Praise of God's Goodness Seen in Creation

Psalm 145:8-11, 148:1-4, 7-14 (ERV)

Leader: We praise you, LORD, for your goodness which is seen in your creation. Your creation reflects your glory, hinting to what is beyond what we can imagine.

Side 1: The LORD is kind and merciful, patient and full of love. The LORD is good to everyone. He shows his mercy to everything he made.

Side 2: LORD, all you have made will praise you. They will tell how great your kingdom is. They will tell how great you are.

Side 1: Praise the LORD! Angels above, praise the LORD from heaven!

Side 2: Praise him, all you angels! Praise him, all his army!

Side 1: Sun and moon, praise him! Stars and lights in the sky, praise him!

Side 2: Praise him, highest heavens, you waters above the heavens.

Side 1: Everything on earth, praise him! Great sea animals and all the oceans, praise the LORD!

Side 2: Praise him, fire and hail, snow and clouds and the stormy winds that obey him.

Side 1: Praise him, mountains and hills, fruit trees and cedar trees.

Side 2: Praise him, wild animals and cattle, reptiles and birds.

Side 1: Praise him, kings of the earth and all nations, princes and all rulers on earth.

Side 2: Praise him, young men and women, old people and children.

Side 1: Praise the LORD'S name! Honor his name forever! His name is greater than any other. He is more glorious than heaven and earth.

Side 2: He made his people strong. His loyal followers praise him. Israel, his precious people, praise the LORD!

All: Hallelujah!

Leader: Glory be to the Father, and to the Son, and to the Holy Spirit,

All: As it was in the beginning, is now, and ever shall be, world without end. Amen.

Question 3: Who Created God?

Background for the Catechist

A student from a family that was quite active in the parish asked this question. She had a look of concern in her eye. She was questioning her family's faith, and had a number of other similar questions as well. This question came up on many other occasions from other students in other classes, although more often in a tone more curious than critical.

God: Not a Being among Beings

Before directly answering the question, I believe it helpful to clarify a likely misunderstanding. Perhaps naturally enough, students are thinking of God as a being among beings in the world – that he is simply the greatest being. The traditional religion of the ancient Greeks, and many other ancient faiths, presented the divine in this way. Also, this question – who created God? – is seriously posed by modern atheists, challenging the popular conception of God as the greatest of beings among beings. Yet the god who is just a being among beings is simply an idol – he is not God (SCG 1.25). We must shake students of this conception both because it is false and because it cannot stand against the anti-religious pressures of our day.

The Christian God is transcendent. The *Merriam-Webster Dictionary* defines transcendent as "extending or lying beyond the limits of ordinary experience." God is also immanent, holding us in existence at every moment. As transcendent, St. Thomas taught that God can only be known by human reason in an analogical way since God is disproportionate to our world – including our minds (SCG 1.32; ST I, 2, 2, ad. 3). This is not to say we can't know anything of God, but that we can only know him in a likeness but not face to face. As St. Paul writes of our knowledge of God, "At present we see indistinctly, as in a mirror, but then face to face. At present I know partially; then I shall know fully, as I am fully known" (1 Cor. 13:12 [NABRE]). As we will see later on, St. Thomas taught that in Heaven, God will give us new vision to see him as he is. (See Question 4: "What Does God Look Like?")

A Necessary Being

All of St. Thomas' Five Ways for the Existence of God (see Question 1: "Does God Really Exist?"), based on effects seen in the world, conclude that for our world to exist, it must go back to one Being who is not dependent on anything else for what it is. In his 3rd Way, St. Thomas taught that there must be a Necessary Being. Things in our direct experience are often coming into being and passing out of being. Clouds come and go, animals are born and die. Scientists even tell us how mountains were formed and how they will eventually be destroyed. But anything for which it would be possible to come into existence or pass from existence does not have the qualifications for the Being which is ultimately responsible for the existence of everything. If everything that *could* not exist *did not* exist, nothing would exist now. There must be a being for whom existence is simply part of what it is, and this Being is God.

For our world to exist, something must have existed prior to bringing it into being. Some atheists believe that the Big Bang is what is ultimately responsible for our world. According to them, in the beginning there was hot, dense **matter** which was about to explode. But this does not explain how this matter got there in the first place. Nothing about this matter implies that it is necessary in any way or that it is completely independent of everything else. Perhaps the Necessary Being created these particles, but our quest for the Necessary Being continues.

What does it mean to be the Necessary Being? It means that its essence is its existence (ST I, 3, 4). An **essence** is what makes a being what it is and which makes up its powers. God's essence is "to be" and he is one with his powers since there is nothing beyond God to be a cause for him. While we participate in being, God does not – he is Existence itself. As God told Moses: "I am who I am" (Exodus 3:14). Likewise, God does not simply know this or that – he is Truth itself. Everything capable of being known ultimately comes from him. There is nothing more fundamental than God. Nothing caused him to be – he is the uncaused Cause. Nothing set him in motion – he is the unmoved Mover. While to us, God's nature may be mysterious, to God, it is clear that it could be no different than it is without beginning or end.

The Necessary Being could not be hot, dense particles not only because particles are the type of things that come into existence and pass from existence, but also because the Necessary Being must be pure Spirit. As Spirit, God is not visible to our eyes, yet he is an Intelligence more real than we ourselves. Anything material is made up of parts that can be rearranged or broken up (ST I, 3, 1). Hence anything material has the potential for change. But God is perfect, so God never changes (ST I, 9, 1). He is **immutable**, so he can never be rearranged, broken up, or even grow. He is the First Mover which itself must be unmoved; this is how movement first was effected in the world (see St. Thomas' 1st Way in Question 1, also ST I, 3, 1). The particles behind the Big Bang were not one but many and they exploded and became other things different from what they once were. Any such things that can change – even more so this *plurality* of particles – are beings for which it was possible not to be (SCG 1.18). They also could not be a first mover but rather something intermediate in the world's chain of movement, even if toward the beginning.

In sum, God is not a being among beings and wasn't created by anyone. For there to be anything in the world now, there had to be a Necessary Being from whom all beings receive their existence. God has the qualities required for a Necessary Being: he is outside this world (**transcendent**), he is one, he is all perfect, he is pure spirit, he is unchanging (immutable), and he is **eternal**. The particles behind the Big Bang cannot be this Necessary Being. To believe that they are the ultimate cause of our world takes more faith and less reason than believing that God is indeed the one who can simply say "I am who I am."

Our Relationship with the Necessary Being

We've emphasized God's transcendence, but our Christian faith balances God's transcendence with God's immanence – that he is closer to us than we are to ourselves. God is Being Itself – he simply is. We, on the other hand, can come and go – we are not necessary beings but "**contingent beings**." We depend in our existence on him at every moment. In his eternal mind, he has his plan of us by which he knows us better than we know ourselves, and by his will he made us to be and holds us in being at all times. God will never forget about us, but if he did, we would cease to exist all together. He is the ground of our being. It is as if our being is "on loan" from him, but on loan forever because he made our souls immortal, inviting us to live with him forever.

Reflection for the Catechist

- o What does it mean to say that God is transcendent, and how do we understand God as not merely a "being among beings?"
- o Do you agree or disagree with this statement: "It takes more faith to believe in Chance than it does to believe in God"? And why?
- o God revealed his Name to Moses: "I AM WHO I AM." In light of St. Thomas' teaching on the Necessary Being, how can we go deeper in understanding the Name of God?
- o St. Thomas points out that we are the type of being from whom it is possible not to be (contingent beings). What implications does this have for our relationship with God and others?

Presentation Ideas

Key concept: God is not a being among other beings. He is the Necessary Being – the Being beyond our world who is responsible for all created beings.

Scripture: "If... the people will ask, 'What is his name?' what should I tell them?" Then God said to Moses, "I AM WHO I AM" - Exodus 3:13-14 (NABRE)

Five Ways for the Existence of God

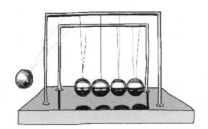

Refer to the presentation ideas for Question 1: "Does God Really Exist?" which shows the need for our world to go back to a Being that is outside this world that doesn't depend on anything. Especially look to the activity for the 1st Way for God's Existence ("Motion"). It uses the motion of a pendulum to show that all motion in the world must have been started from a First Mover outside the world. Also consider the activity for the 2nd Way for God's Existence ("The Coming-To-Be of Things"). It involves tracing the causes of familiar things back to God.

God Is and Could Be No Other Way

> **Activity #1:** Explain to the students: we are familiar with beings existing but eventually not existing any more. Think of a tree which grows from a seed and eventually dies. But if everything were like this, then nothing would exist now. (It would then be possible for everything not to exist).

> Explanation: There has to be a Being who just is and who could be no other way. In fact, God revealed himself as just such a Being.

> **Activity #2:** Next give groups of students five popsicle sticks per group (any rigid stick will do). Have a ruler available. Tell the students to make a square or rectangle (with 90° angles) using four of the sticks. Then fix the fifth stick across from one corner of the rectangle to the other such that the distance across is less than any of the sides of the rectangle. Have the students try for a short period of time and measure the sides of their figure with a ruler. The task is impossible. If the students already know it's impossible, ask them just to try once or twice to see for themselves. (This activity could also be done on a blackboard.)

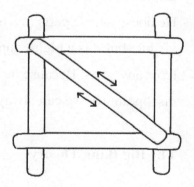

> Symbols: This rule of geometry – i.e. that the hypotenuse of a triangle is always longer than its sides – represents how God likewise just is and could not be different.

> Explanation: It is a necessary principle that when you go across any square or rectangle from one corner to the other, that straight line (the **hypotenuse**) is always longer than any of the sides. In a similar way, God could be no other way. He simply is. In fact, the rules of geometry are grounded in him. People may debate about what God is like. But to God, his own necessity is clear.

God as Spirit

Activity: Bring in a twig with several branches. Ask the students whether a twig could be the type of being that could be no other way. Point out the different branches and how they could have grown in other directions, how the color could have been different, or how there may or may not be leaves on it. Break off part of the twig. Show how it is easily changed and easily turned into something else. Ask what it is turned into if burned.

Symbols: The twig – growing in different directions, having or not having leaves, and able to be snapped in two – represents what God is *not* like. God is **simple**, meaning without parts that can be broken or rearranged.

Explanation: God, as the Necessary Being, cannot be like the twig that grows either this way or that way. He doesn't have parts (even the Trinity are not parts but *relations* within God). He is Spirit. Spirit is not visible, but it is a highly intelligent power that is very real. You can't break Spirit up because it doesn't have any parts. Because he is Spirit and is all good, God never changes. That's why even when people disappoint us, we can always place our trust in God.

The Big Bang Theory

Discussion: Older students may be familiar with the Big Bang theory. Some people see that as an alternative to God as Creator. Make a chart (see below) and explain that the Necessary Being – the Being who simply is – must be the following. He must be one, beyond the world (transcendent), pure spirit, unchanging, and eternal. Behind the "Big Bang" were hot, dense particles. Explain that these particles don't qualify as the Necessary Being. One must ask how they got there in the first place.

	One	Beyond the World	Spirit	Unchanging	Eternal
God	✓	✓	✓	✓	✓
"Big Bang" Particles					

Requirements for the Necessary Being

Explanation: The Necessary Being must be:

- **One:** because if it were many it could have been different
- **Beyond the world / transcendent:** because the Necessary Being is existence itself, and because the world cannot set itself in motion
- **Spirit:** because only spirit can forever remain the same and not change
- **Eternal:** because only a being with no beginning or end can be ultimately responsible for everything

The particles are none of these. They are many, they are material, they change, and they cease to exist as such. If these particles ever existed, they must have been created by God, the Necessary Being. It takes more faith to believe these particles are the *ultimate* cause of our existence than to believe in God, the Necessary Being.

What It Means to Say God Is Beyond the World

Activity: Draw a very small circle on the blackboard and say it represents Earth and other relatively small circles to represent planets. Ask the students if they know the names of some other planets. Then ask the students how big God would be in proportion to these planets. Work toward the idea that we shouldn't even draw God on the blackboard at all. He is everywhere and also beyond. He is more like the air that fills the room and the skies above.

Symbols: The circles drawn on the blackboard represent Earth and the other planets. The air – which fills the room and the sky – represents God, who is unimaginably beyond the little dots on the blackboard.

Explanation: Earth and the other planets – as big as they are – are nothing compared to God. They are just like a drop in the ocean. No one can even weigh or measure God. He is beyond all that. Likewise, God isn't just one of the beings in our world that needed to be created. He is beyond our world, and he is the one being that just *is*. Without him, there could never be anything else.

Review

Split students into groups, with each group explaining one of these topics before the class:

- How God is different from other beings.
- What it means to say God is Spirit.
- Why the Big Bang theory doesn't discredit God.

Meditation from the Confessions of St. Augustine

The Confessions of St. Augustine, Modern English Version, 17-19

Reader 1:

You are matchless, O Lord.

So our praise of You must rise above our humanity.

Magnificent is Your power.

Your wisdom has no limits.

And we lowly creatures aspire to praise You. What is a human being, but a tiny particle of Your creation? ...

Reader 2:

For who is Lord but the Lord?

Who is God except our God?

The highest.

The most good.

The most mighty.

The most omnipotent.

The most merciful, yet most just.

The most hidden, yet most present.

The most beautiful, yet strongest....

Reader 3:

And what have I now said, my God, my life, my holy joy? What does any mortal say when speaking of You? Yet woe to the one who does not speak, for silence is the most eloquent voice.

Oh, that I might rest on You.

Oh, that You would enter my heart... so that I might forget all woes and embrace You, my only good.

Amen.

Question 4: What Does God Look Like?

Background for the Catechist

A story goes that a teacher walked around the classroom and asked the children what they were drawing. One child told her, "I'm drawing God." The teacher said, "But no one knows what God looks like," to which the child replied, "Well, now they will!"

According to 1st John 4:12, "No one has ever seen God" (NABRE). Exodus 33:23 tells us that the Lord passed before Moses; he showed Moses his back but would not show him his face "for no one can see me and live" (Ex. 33:20 [NABRE]). St. Thomas tells us that language such as this speaking of God's "back" and his "face" is metaphorical (ST I, 3, 1). God is pure Spirit and does not have a **body** – although, as we will discuss later, he became man in Jesus. But now we are speaking of God as God – what we call the divine nature.

God cannot be seen with physical eyes, and yet we will indeed "see" God in Heaven. Allow me to explain. The most beautiful and the most real vision we could ever have is not of something visible to eyes at all – in fact it is something that we need "superpowers" in order to grasp. It is what St. Thomas called the **Beatific Vision** – the vision of God.

The Beatific Vision

God is infinite goodness, truth, love, etc. We will never exhaust the vision of God, but as Peter Kreeft, a follower of St. Thomas' thought, says, it will be like exploring in wonder and delight (*Everything You Ever Wanted to Know About Heaven*, 52-53). We will not just imagine it, but we will have real spiritual vision of it. And it will thoroughly delight us because God will prepare us and purify our desires for it.

Recall from Question 2 that for all eternity God knows and loves himself in the Trinity. Well, only God can naturally know himself as he really is (his "essence"). Just as a bat cannot see in the daylight, so our minds – and even the minds of angels – cannot grasp God as he is (SCG 3.53). But in Heaven, God will give us, just as he gave the faithful angels, spiritual "**supernatural**" sight to see him. Only God can grant that gift, and only this can satisfy all our desires which he created. And because of this gift, for all eternity

27

we will see his "face" which he withheld from Moses on Mount Sinai. This represents God as he really is. Anyone who sees God in this way can never return because it completely fulfills every desire, leaving no room for wishing any lesser thing (SCG 3.62).

What We Will See in Heaven

With spiritual vision – not our physical eyes – we will see God in Heaven as he really is, for spirit is highly intelligible (ST Supplement III, 92, 2). God will both be what we see and the means by which we see. We will also have physical eyes and will see beautiful things with them – and our spiritual vision of God will make us to see these things with the **beauty** that God sees them. We will see Jesus face to face with our physical eyes – and his glorified body will be the most beautiful physical sight in Heaven. We will also see the glorified bodies of all the saints.

The Meaning of "Spiritual Vision"

Each fall in our faith formation program, we take our 6th graders to the nearby Basilica of Our Lady of Victory in Lackawanna, NY – the grandest and most beautiful church in our area. Each year, the students get off the bus and gather in the back foyer before the great wooden doors of the church. The tour guide points out many interesting historical facts and astounding architectural figures. But when he or she opens the great doors and the students behold their first sight of the beauty, the expanse, the harmony, the grandness of the interior of the sanctuary, the students gasp with wonder and awe. This is not about any curious or interesting fact or even anything merely pretty or enjoyable, but is a hint of the eternal spiritual vision we will have of the beauty of God himself. This created harmony is an intimation and a participation in God who is Goodness, Truth, and Beauty itself. In our spiritual vision of God, we will not simply behold beautiful or good things, but will behold the very Goodness, Truth, and Beauty by which those things register in our minds as good, true, or beautiful. And everything in Heaven that we see with our physical eyes will be illuminated by that spiritual vision.

Goodness, Truth, and Beauty

For St. Thomas, everything that exists – everything whatsoever – has certain goodness, truth, and beauty which reflects God (ST I, 5, 1; ST 44, 1; Disputed Questions on Truth 1.1). As good, all beings are in some way desirable by the will. As true, all beings are in some way able to be understood by the mind. As beautiful, all beings have a certain harmony which is pleasant to the mind (ST 1, 5, 4, ad. 1). Think of the basilica I mentioned above. It was good – we all found it very attractive and were glad to find that such things still exist. It was true – we were able to understand its purpose and structure, which were placed at the service of the Christian community. It was beautiful – its harmony was apparent to all and pleasing in a way that was beyond the mere "pretty."

But if all beings are good, true, and beautiful, then why are we (rightly) turned off by evil beings? Because **evil** is like a parasite on being – it takes away more or less of its goodness, truth, and beauty. But nothing – not even Satan himself – is so far gone that it is deprived of all goodness, truth, and beauty. Just as a parasite dies without its host, evil needs at least some goodness for it to corrupt since it is simply the absence of a due good (SCG 3.11). We will discuss this more later on.

Clarification: Created in the Image of God

It is a fundamental truth that our dignity as human persons arises from our being created in the **image of God**. But what does this mean, now that we see that we cannot "look" like God? It means that as God knows and loves, so we are given the capacity to know and love God and each other (ST I, 3, 1, ad. 1). This capacity leads us towards the spiritual vision of God in Heaven, where we will be immersed in God's infinite knowledge and love.

Reflection for the Catechist

- Recall an "ah ha" moment in which you "saw" an idea with the eye of the mind. What was it, and with what clarity did you "see" it?
- In what way will the spiritual vision of God in Heaven make everything else we see in Heaven appear all the more beautiful?

- o God told Moses that he could show him his back but not his face. Since God isn't a body, what does his "back" and "face" possibly represent? How does it relate to the Beatific Vision, or the spiritual vision of God in Heaven?

- o What exactly is goodness, truth, and beauty? What difference does it make to us and our world that God is Goodness, Truth, and Beauty itself?

- o How do you experience God's transcendence in goodness? in truth? in beauty? Which one do you gravitate to the most?

Presentation Ideas

Key concept: No one can see God with their eyes because he is Spirit. But in Heaven, God will give us spiritual vision with which to see him as he is. He is Goodness, Truth, and Beauty Itself. We will explore his mysteries forever in wonder and awe. With our eyes, we will see Jesus and the saints. Our spiritual vision of God will make them even more beautiful.

Scripture: "God is Spirit. So the people who worship him must worship in spirit and truth."
     – Jesus in John 4:24 (ERV)

Spiritual Vision

 **Activity:** Ask the students if they have ever watched a movie with 3D glasses. Perhaps have a pair of 3D glasses for students to try on. The 3D movie can only be seen in 3D if you have your 3D glasses on. Without the 3D glasses, the movie doesn't appear in 3D.

Symbols: The 3D glasses represent the gift God will give us in Heaven to see him spiritually as he is. The movie in 3D represents what God "looks" like. But without the glasses, the movie can't be seen in 3D.

Explanation: We aren't prepared now to see God as he is. But he will give us this vision in Heaven. In Heaven, we will have our eyes back someday. But that's not how we will see God. Our eyes are made for seeing physical things. But God is not physical but spiritual. So in Heaven, God will give us "spiritual vision" to see him because he is pure Spirit. We don't know exactly what God "looks" like. We do have hints, though, and we know he is very beautiful. (For an explanation of what it means to say God is "Spirit," see Question 3: "Who Created God?")

Goodness, Truth, and Beauty: Hints of God's Glory

Even though we don't see God with our eyes, we have hints of what God "looks like." This is because everything he made reflects him. Three qualities in all things especially reflect God: goodness, truth, and beauty.

Goodness

Activity: Have the students think of something good – like a friend. Friends are good – they accept us as we are and are companions in many things we do. But different friends are good in different ways. One friend is an especially good listener and is very kind. Another friend is a lot of fun and makes people feel good. Still another friend is bold and creative and leads the way.

Explanation: We can say that goodness is that which God created our desires to be satisfied by. The examples above are things that reflect God's goodness. But God is not just good in this way or that way. He is Goodness Itself. He's where all goodness comes from. He's so good that if we saw him, he would be literally and completely irresistible!

Truth

Activity #1: By "truth" we mean anything that can be understood by a mind. Students have many questions. In gazing into God in Heaven someday, we will find the answers to everything we want to know. In fact, everything our minds know is a reflection of God, who is Truth itself. Ask the students: What would you ask God if you could ask him about anything?

Activity #2: Ask the students to recall a moment they were working on a difficult school project and finally figured out the answer. What is that moment like, when everything "clicks"? That's what it's like when our minds discover the truth. In the end, all truth comes from God. Ask: What do you think it would be like to see all that truth in an instant in Heaven someday?

Beauty

Activity: Have the students think about something beautiful, like a sunset. Ask them what color sunsets they like the best – red, orange, purple, pink, etc. Or ask what they like to see sunsets over – the sea, a mountain, a lake, a winter scene, etc. But one sunset scene is not another. They are all beautiful in their own way. A red sunset scene is not the same as a purple one. One over a lake is not the same sight as a sunset over a snowy hill. This sunset is beautiful in one way, while another sunset is beautiful in another way.

Explanation: Beauty is that which is pleasing not only to our eyes but especially to our spirit or mind because of its order and harmony. Every sunset, for example, is beautiful in a different way. But each reflects God, who is Beauty Itself.

What We Will See in Heaven

Explain to the students: in Heaven, we will have physical eyes. With those eyes, we will see Jesus, and the saints. This includes friends and family. With our spiritual vision, we will see God. This spiritual vision of God will also help us to see everything as God sees it. This will make everything even more beautiful to us!

Activity for Younger Students: Ask the students if anyone has ever gone swimming and opened their eyes under water. Everything is blurry and your eyes hurt. But when you have goggles, you can swim up to everything and comfortably see it as it really is.

Symbols: Looking underwater without goggles represents how we see the world now. Looking underwater with goggles represents how we will see everything after we have the spiritual vision of God in Heaven.

Explanation: Sometimes we don't see the good in people. It's like looking without goggles under water. But in Heaven, we always will see people as God sees them – with goodness and beauty. God sees us as we really are, and we will see other people the way God sees them. We will see clearly how they reflect him.

Activity for Older Students: When you love someone, you see the good in them in a way that other people do not.

Explanation: God is in love with us. He sees all the good in us. In Heaven, we will see other people as God sees them and we will live in friendship and harmony with all. We will see all things as a lover sees them, and we will see how they reflect God.

Review

Have the students draw a picture or make a collage to represent what God is like. Have the students explain the symbols to the class.

Meditation: Think about What Is Good

Philippians 4:8-9 (ERV)

Brothers and sisters, continue to think about what is good and worthy of praise. Think about what is true and honorable and right and pure and beautiful and respected. And do what you learned and received from me – what I told you and what you saw me do. And the God who gives peace will be with you.

Question 5: How Big Is God and Where Is He?

Background for the Catechist

Two of God's attributes in particular stand as the answer to these questions. The answer to "how big is God?" is that God is infinite (without end). The answer to "where is he?" is that he is omnipresent (present everywhere). In fact, the way the student phrased this question is exactly the order St. Thomas wrote about it in the *Summa Theologica*. As we may see now, God's attributes are connected to one another. In fact, for St. Thomas, these two attributes presuppose another attribute: God's goodness.

God's Goodness, Infinity, and Omnipresence

St. Thomas' thinking flows a little like this. An intelligent Creator is greater and more perfect than what he creates, so God is the highest good (ST I, 6, 1). Everything God created is good within its bounds: a human is good as a human, a horse is good as a horse, and a human's good is not realized if it acts like a horse. But since God is the first cause of all created things, he is not himself placed within any bounds, nor could he be since he exists of himself (ST I, 7, 1). Only infinite goodness and being could have the power to bring creation into being from not being at all. So we understand God's Being to be infinite, which likewise implies his **omnipresence** – that he is in all things and present to all things, but is closed in by nothing.

"How Big Is God and Where Is He?"

Let's try to answer how "big" God is. Say we wanted to try to compare God to the Empire State Building. It's not simply that God is infinitely "bigger" than the Empire State Building. The Empire State Building is made out of steel and other materials that can be measured. God is pure Spirit, so he is not stretched out in space and is not limited by space.

Further, we might ask "where is God?" Well, God is not subject to space. But all things that are in space are held in existence by God. For St. Thomas, a spirit "is" where it acts (ST I, 8, 1, *sed contra*). And since

God holds all things in existence, he is "in" all things as the ground of their being. This is what we mean by God's omnipresence. He is everywhere, and also beyond.

God's Immanence

God is present in things in different ways. This is what we mean by saying that God is "immanent." St. Thomas teaches that God is everywhere by being, by presence, and by power (ST I, 8, 3). This also makes clear that while God is in all things, there is a distinction between God and his creation.

- By being, God is the cause of all created being, holding it in existence at every moment because only he is Being itself. In this way he is in all things as the ground of their being. God will never forget about us, but if he did, we would cease to exist.
- By presence, God has constant knowledge and love of the creation he holds in existence. Actually as our Creator, God's knowledge and plan of us is the cause of our being (ST I, 14, 8). That's why God knows us better than we know ourselves. God is in the soul of a Christian (in the state of grace) in an even more special way – by grace through a special and familiar indwelling by which we become sons and daughters of God (ST I, 8, 3).
- By power, he is present to all creation by his providential care. We will discuss this more later.

God is also in Heaven, but Heaven does not contain him. In Heaven, his will is done perfectly and everything is ordered to him perfectly. His being, presence, and power there is indeed felt the most strongly.

Attributes of God

By now, the students' questions have led us to stumble upon a number of God's attributes. In this following chart, let's take a look at some of the attributes of God as St. Thomas presents them toward the beginning of his *Summa Theologica*:

God's Attributes	Meaning
Simple	Pure Spirit (immaterial intelligence), not having a body and thus not made up of parts (see Question 3: "Who Created God?") (ST I, 3, 1).
All Perfect & Good	Having all perfection and desirable in every way (see Question 1: "Does God Really Exist?") (ST I, 6, 2).
Infinite	Without end or limit in being. This follows on God's being good without limit (ST I, 7, 1).
Omnipresent	Present to all he has made. But because he is Spirit, we don't mean stretched out infinitely in space (ST I, 8, 1).
Immutable	Cannot be harmed or destroyed in any way. Because God is simple, in the sense of "spiritual," he is also immutable (see Question 3: "Who Created God?") (ST I, 9, 1).
Eternal	Existing (outside of time) without beginning or end. Only God has no beginning and is thus eternal in the full sense of the word. God's immutability implies his eternity (ST I, 10, 2).
Omniscient	Having ultimate knowledge of all things. That God has knowledge follows from God's being simple, or spiritual. Since he is infinite, he has infinite knowledge (ST I, 14, 12).
Omnipotent	Having power to do all that is possible to do. This follows on God's goodness and infinity (ST I, 25, 3).

Reflection for the Catechist

- ○ Is God "big" in the same sense that the Empire State Building is big? How is God's infinity different from physical size?
- ○ Identify these terms with regard to God's attributes: simple, good, infinite, omnipresent, immutable, eternal, omniscient, omnipotent.
- ○ How do God's attributes imply one another? For example, how does God's goodness imply his infinity and his infinity imply his omnipresence?
- ○ What is the difference between saying that God is in all things (as a Christian does) and God *is* all things (as a **Pantheist** does)? What difference does it make?
- ○ What implications does God's infinity and omnipresence have for our life of prayer and our trust in God? How about God's other attributes?

Presentation Ideas

Key Concept: God's Spirit is in all the created things in the world holding them in being. But God is not limited to the world. He is infinite, or without limit. He is also omnipresent, or everywhere. He is not contained by Heaven or by the universe.

Scripture: "Your Spirit is everywhere I go. I cannot escape your presence." – Psalm 139:7 (ERV)

God: Beyond Everything

Refer to the activity "God: Beyond Everything" in the Presentation Ideas for Question 3: "Who Created God?" It is an activity that seeks to impress the concept that God is both bigger than the universe and beyond it. The activity involves imagining God in relation to the planets. Refer also to the activity "God as Spirit," also under Question 3.

God Holds Creation in Being

Instruction: Have the students think about something they have made. What is it?

Discussion: There is a big difference between what we make and what God creates. We make things from other things. When God creates, he creates out of nothing. *He* is the Source of its being. In order for something created from nothing to continue existing, God must continue holding it in existence. Since God created everything, he holds everything in existence. Thus God is everywhere – with every thing – and beyond our Universe as well. This is called **omnipresence**.

Further: Because he made all things and is in all things, he knows all things. He is also in Heaven, but Heaven does not contain him.

How Big Is God and Where Is He?

Activity #1: Have the students think about a thing – any thing. Ask them what it is – i.e. a tree, a dog, a cloud, a person, a house, a planet, etc.

Explanation: Tell the students that God is not any created thing. Instead, he is in each of those things as the One who constantly makes them to exist. There is nothing that escapes God's reach. If the thing the students are thinking of doesn't really exist, God is still thinking about it. God is in all things, but he is also beyond all things. He is infinite – limited by nothing.

Activity #2: Have the students think of something really big – the Empire State Building. The Empire State Building is in New York City. It is not in Chicago. But as infinite Spirit, God is in both New York and Chicago in the same way, holding everything in being. Also, the air is everywhere on earth, but the same air is not on a far away planet. Still, God is in that planet in the same way, holding it in existence.

Infinity

Activity: For older students, give them about two minutes to divide 8 by 9 on paper without rounding or stopping. Eight is infinitely divisible by 9. As it turns out, $8 / 9 = 0.88888....$

Explanation: If we didn't stop at 2 minutes, students could go on forever. *Infinity* goes on forever without end. In division, sometimes we can divide infinitely, moving towards a very small, precise number. God's infinity, though, is a positive infinity of goodness, perfection, and being. This is goodness without end. This goodness is the Source of our being.

God Is in Our Hearts

Activity #1: Explain to the students that when we are in the state of grace, God is present to us not only as holding us in existence but also as living in our hearts in a special way. Read the following excerpt from the "St. Patrick's Breastplate Prayer." Ask the students what it must have meant to St. Patrick that God was everywhere and especially within him. Also ask the students what it means to them.

> Christ be with me, Christ within me,
> Christ behind me, Christ before me,
> Christ beside me, Christ to win me,
> Christ to comfort and restore me.
> Christ beneath me, Christ above me,
> Christ in quiet, Christ in danger,
> Christ in hearts of all that love me,
> Christ in mouth of friend and stranger.

Activity #2: Have students draw a picture or make a collage on the theme of St. Patrick's Breastplate. Ask them to explain the artwork.

Review

Pair up students to explain an answer to "how big is God and where is he?"

Prayer Service: God's Closeness to Us at All Times

Psalm 139:1-14 (ERV)

Side 1: Lord, you have tested me, so you know all about me. You know when I sit down and when I get up. You know my thoughts from far away.

Side 2: You know where I go and where I lie down. You know everything I do. LORD, you know what I want to say, even before the words leave my mouth.

Side 1: You are all around me – in front of me and behind me. I feel your hand on my shoulder. I am amazed at what you know; it is too much for me to understand.

Side 2: Your Spirit is everywhere I go. I cannot escape your presence.

Side 1: If I go up to heaven, you will be there. If I go down to the place of death, you will be there.

Side 2: If I go east where the sun rises or go to live in the west beyond the sea, even there you will take my hand and lead me. Your strong right hand will protect me.

Side 1: Suppose I wanted to hide from you and said, "Surely the darkness will hide me. The day will change to night and cover me." Even the darkness is not dark to you. The night is as bright as the day. Darkness and light are the same.

Side 2: You formed the way I think and feel. You put me together in my mother's womb. I praise you because you made me in such a wonderful way.

All: Amen.

Question 6: How Does God Rule Creation?

Background for the Catechist

The students know that God is a King, but what does that really mean? Some people – the Deists, for example – believe like us that God created everything, but they believe it stops there – that he leaves his creation completely to its own devices until the end of time. But as Christians, we believe that God is always concerned for his creation and likewise intervenes in history. We believe that God rules over all creation by his **providence**, which means his "foresight."

God's Providence: The Order and Purpose within Creation

St. Thomas teaches that providence involves two things, which are related. First it means that as Designer, God created everything with purpose, ordering all creation to himself (ST I, 22, 3) (Recall the Fifth Way for God's existence in Question 1: "Does God Really Exist?"). He likewise gave all things the **natural powers** to reach the ends or purposes he designed them for. As the one who holds all things in existence, he likewise enables creatures to exercise their powers and provided things their powers correspond to. For example, when we love our friend, we may be living according to God's design for the human loves. And God's foresight saw to it that we have the ability to love and that our friend be good to draw our love. But this has to do with God's plan of goodness from the beginning of creation, so as Christians, we believe still more about God's providence that builds on this.

God's Providence: Governance of All Events

The second meaning of God's providence relates to his governance of all creation – his ordering of all events that happen in creation to a greater good. In the Gospel, Jesus reminds us, "If God so clothes the grass of the field, which grows today and is thrown into the oven tomorrow, will he not much more provide for you, O you of little faith?" (Mt. 6:30 [NABRE]).

God orders all events to the greater good in such a way that protects free will, allows for events to befall as they will in most circumstances, and works either through secondary causes or directly. Let's discuss these points below:

43

God Preserves Free Will. God ensures people's free will even if their choice is for sin or evil because people can only truly love if they love freely (SCG 3.73). And remember, God created us to know, love, and serve him (see Question 2: "Why did God Create the World?"). God is not responsible for people's bad choices, however, nor does he condone them. For now, God gives us the **law** and also grace to follow it, but in the end, God will judge so as to order all things to goodness.

God Works Either Directly or through Secondary Causes. God can always intervene directly in creation and history when he wishes (such as miracles), but often he allows events to unfold through the working of creatures. For example, scientists tell us mountains were formed through the shifting of the earth's crust. This does not mean that God did not create the mountains, but that he used **secondary causes** in their formation. St. Thomas tells us that the reason God often works through secondary causes is to give creatures – and especially people – their place in shaping the events of history (ST I, 22, 3). For example, God doesn't usually infuse knowledge of math and science into our heads – we learn through books and teachers, and in that God grants us knowledge.

God Decides Whether Events Happen Necessarily or Contingently (fall as they will). When you roll a die in a board game, there is a 1:6 chance of getting your desired number – so clearly God allows many things to fall as they will through their "secondary causes." But sometimes God wills that something happens necessarily and without fail (SCG 3.75). For example, when the Apostles chose who would replace Judas as an Apostle in the Book of Acts, they prayed to the Holy Spirit and the lots fell to Matthias (Acts 1:26). This happened by God's will. We don't always know for certain whether a particular event came from God necessarily or whether he simply allowed it to take place, but in the case of God's acting in Scripture and Tradition, the Church marks out certain events as coming necessarily from him. We also know that the evil of sin is something that God allows to fall as it comes from a person's free will.

God Works All Events for the Universal Good

St. Paul tells us, "We know that all things work for good for those who love God, who are called according to his purpose" (Rom. 8:28 [NABRE]). The closer we are to God, the more God intervenes in our lives, and the closer still we draw to him. St. Paul's guarantee, however, is to "those who love God." For those who do not love God, all things still work for the greater good of God's creation (SCG 3.71).

Still, God allows people to do great evil so that goodness may battle it and grow even stronger. For example, as St. Thomas teaches, if there were no persecution, there would be no virtue of patience. If there were no crimes, there would be no restorative justice (SCG 3.75). These examples are of moral evil. Natural evil – such as natural disasters, illness, or physical suffering – are a consequence of **Original Sin** but not necessarily personal sin. Sometimes when great evil happens, we will never know how God ordered it to the greater good until he shows us in Heaven. We may wonder why God permits evil to happen in our world, but the *Catechism of the Catholic Church* tells us that on this side of Heaven, "Only Christian faith as a whole constitutes the answer to this question" (CCC no. 309).

Reflection for the Catechist

- How is God's providence built into creatures themselves? (See the second paragraph.)
- What are secondary causes, and how does God work through them? Are they necessary for God to work?
- Christians profess that creation is from God. Atheists contend that evolution is by chance. How might an understanding of secondary causes bring light to the discussion on evolution?
- Why does God allow people to commit evil? How does it tie into his providential plan?
- How might we understand natural disasters in light of the principles concerning God's providence? Also, what does it mean to say that "only Christian faith as a whole constitutes the answer" to the problem of evil?
- What does it mean to entrust oneself to God's providence?

Presentation Ideas

Key concept: God rules creation by his "providence," or foresight, in two ways. First, he provides for all things by what he gave them in creation and how he preserves them. Second, he directs all events for the greater good. He does this in a way that respects our freedom. He works sometimes through other creatures. He also decides when to let things happen by themselves and when to make sure they happen for certain.

Scripture: "Are not two sparrows sold for a small coin? Yet not one of them falls to the ground without your Father's knowledge." – Jesus in Matthew 10:29 (NABRE)

The Designer's Care in Providing What We Need

Activity: Show the students a bird's nest or a picture of a bird's nest. Have students describe it and tell how it serves its purpose. Imagine how it may have been built.

Reflection: The nest was built by a bird – a creature with instinct but not intelligence. Most of the nests built by the same species will be very similar because of this instinct, which is triggered by certain events. God gave the bird species this instinct to make nests so that they would be able to survive and take care of their young.

Explanation: God gives every type of creature what it needs to thrive. He gives birds the instinct to build nests. He gives fish fins with which to swim. He gives humans a mind in order to think. He also holds these creatures and their powers in existence at every moment. This is the first way God rules creation, but not the only way.

God Directs All Events for the Greater Good

Activity: Have the students look up and read Romans 8:28: "We know that in everything God works for the good of those who love him" (ERV).

Explanation: This verse from the Bible tells us that no matter what, God is in control. Bad things happen, but God arranges even those things for good. We may never know exactly how until we get to Heaven, though.

Principles for How God Rules the World

Activity: write these principles on the board by which God's governs creation:
- Always respects our free will
- Works either directly or through creatures
- Determines whether to make something happen or simply to allow it to happen

Explanation:

God Always Respects Our Free Will

Explain to the students that God wants us to love him. But in order to love, we need to be free to choose. This also means we have to be free to make bad choices. God allows us to make bad choices but is not responsible for them.

God Works Either Directly or through Creatures

Activity #1. Show the students a picture of balls lying on a pool table. The point of the game is for the player to shoot all the balls into the pockets. But the player doesn't shoot them directly. He uses the stick to hit the white ball which in turn hits another balls, which might hit another ball yet.

Symbols. The player represents God. Using the stick and the white ball to hit the other balls represents how God often works through creatures (called "secondary causes").

Application. If we believe that God created the mountains but scientists tell us that the mountains were formed by movements of the earth's crust, there is not necessarily any contradiction there. God could have used the movements in the earth's crust over time to form the mountains.

Activity #2: Ask the students how God gives us knowledge. He doesn't usually give us knowledge directly. He could, such as when he gives someone a prophecy. But usually God gives us knowledge through books, teachers, or experience. Yet ultimately, all knowledge comes from God because he is the ultimate cause of anything we can learn the truth about. He also gave us minds with which we know them.

Explanation: While God always can act directly, most of the time he acts through people, things, and events.

God Determines Whether to *Make* Something Happen or Simply to *Allow* It to Happen

Sometimes God *makes* something happen for certain. For example, imagine that someone prayed and as a result of that prayer, a person was healed. In that case God made certain that the person was healed – either directly by a miracle or through the doctor's help.

Other times God *allows* events to happen as they will

Activity #1. Select a student to cast dice while other students call out what total they think it will be.

Explanation: When we roll the dice, this usually works by chance. God allows many things to fall as they will. By his wise choice, he decides which events will happen for certain and which ones will happen as they will. But he is always in control.

Activity #2. Point out to the students that we always hear about a lot of bad things happening in the news. Tornadoes, for example, may be spawned in the Midwestern United States.

Explanation: As a general punishment on the world because of Original Sin, nature has been disrupted and bad things sometimes happen. God didn't necessarily send a tornado to punish a particular family whose home was destroyed by the tornado. But God does allow it to happen, and brings about a greater good out of it.

Further explanation: We may never know exactly why God allowed a particular bad event to happen until we get to Heaven, but we can guess. For example, perhaps this loss made the family stronger and less reliant on material things. If a good person died, perhaps it was because God knew they were ready for Heaven at that very time. Still God did not *make* it happen but *allowed* it to happen somehow.

Review

Ask students to define "providence." What are two ways God shows his providence?

Based on the principles on the board, have the students come up with how the following situations might fall under God's providence:

- An answered prayer. How might God have answered it?
- A sin committed. Did God will that?
- Winning a board game. How might God have willed it?
- Recovering under medical care. How do we say God brought the healing?

Meditation: Relying on God's Care

Luke 12:22-31 (ERV)

Reader 1: "Jesus said to his followers, 'So I tell you, don't worry about the things you need to live – what you will eat or what you will wear. Life is more important than food, and the body is more important that what you put on it. Look at the birds. They don't plan, harvest, or save food in houses or barns, but God feeds them. And you are worth much more than crows. None of you can add any time to your life by worrying about it. And if you can't do the little things, why worry about the big things?

Reader 2: "Think about how the wildflowers grow. They don't work or make clothes for themselves. But I tell you that even Solomon, the great and rich king, was not dressed as beautifully as one of these flowers. If God makes what grows in the field so beautiful, what do you think he will do for you? That's just grass – one day it's alive, and the next day someone throws it into a fire. But God cares enough to make it beautiful. Surely he will do much more for you. Your faith is so small!

Reader 3: "So don't worry about what you will eat or what you will drink. Don't worry about it. That's what all those people who don't know God are always thinking about. But your Father knows that you need these things. What you should be thinking about is God's kingdom. Then he will give you all these other things you need."

Question 7: If God Created Everything, Did God Create Evil?

Background for the Catechist

The young student asking this question has stumbled upon what philosophers call "the problem of evil" – an issue that St. Thomas, following St. Augustine, took very seriously. Some people ask, "If God is all good and all powerful, how can evil exist?" How can there be so much poverty in Africa that many children die parentless, without food, and with disease and malnutrition? How is it possible that child molesters are allowed to ruin the lives of so many, and sometimes live their lives with the esteem of society without ever being found out? Certainly, some say, an all good and all powerful God would prevent such things from happening in his world. Some even say that since we all know that there is this kind of evil in the world, a God such as Christians believe in must not exist.

Original Sin and Its Consequences

In the book of Genesis, we see that God created man and woman as the high point of the creatures on earth (Genesis 1:26). This is because he desired for them as rational creatures to know him, love him, and serve him (see Question 2: "Why Did God Create the World?"). Yet there is no real love without freedom, and that involves the freedom to say no. Our first parents chose to reject God by eating the forbidden fruit and instead to selfishly seek happiness in pride (Genesis 3). Because of this first sin, human nature was disrupted and humans became subject to all sorts of evils. Even nature was disrupted. We read in Genesis 3:17-18:

> Cursed is the ground because of you!
>> In toil you shall eat its yield
>> all the days of your life.
> Thorns and thistles it shall bear for you,
>> and you shall eat the grass of the field.
> By the sweat of your brow
>> you shall eat bread,
> Until you return to the ground,

from which you were taken;

For you are dust,

and to dust you shall return (NABRE).

St. Augustine formulated the doctrine of "Original Sin" by interpreting the story of the Fall of Adam and Eve. Original Sin is transmitted to all humans and means we are all born without **sanctifying grace**, the gift of God's dwelling in our hearts which is necessary for salvation. Furthermore we are subject to ignorance about the important things in life, our wills have a tendency to malice, our desires are disrupted by **concupiscence** (not being ordered to reason), and our bodies are subject to weakness, sickness, and death. Notice that all these things involve taking away part of the fullness that God gave to humans and originally intended for them. All in all, the transmission of Original Sin is a terrible thing, but so is the sin of Adam and Eve and of all of us against God. But this is why Jesus came to save us. Furthermore, in baptism we are freed from Original Sin and again have friendship with God. But we are not automatically freed of its consequences – we must always struggle against evil in this life until we arrive in Heaven. We now undergo temptations to sin from the world, the flesh, and the **devil**. The matter is complicated further when we realize that sin leads to more sin.

Two Types of Evil: Fault and Punishment

St. Thomas distinguished between two types of "evil" – fault and punishment (ST I, 48, 6). Think back to Adam and Eve's sin of disobedience and pride in eating the fruit that God forbade them to eat. That was the kind of evil called "fault." As a consequence, God took away certain gifts from them. He took away his presence; he took away the wisdom he gave them; he took away the order that had guided them; and he took away their immunity from many physical evils. That was the evil called "punishment." The evil of fault is a terrible thing, especially considering that sin is an offense against God who is infinitely good and deserving of our love. But punishment is actually a way that goodness seeks to restore itself in the face of the evil of fault.

Now God governs all events in the world in different ways (see Question 6: "How Does God Rule the World?"). As for the evil of fault, God never wills that – he only permits that people be allowed to do what they will even if that means they choose evil. And God himself is all good – he would never do anything that is against the good because it would be against his nature. But God sometimes does will punishment because the purpose of punishment is to rectify an evil and order it back to goodness. Sometimes he wills punishment to happen for certain – as when he took away his gifts from Adam and Eve and their descendants. The Bible also tells us of certain times that God sent punishments on certain people or nations. But other times, God allows for various consequences of Original Sin to fall as they will. As Jesus said, "...those eighteen people who were killed when the tower at Siloam fell on them – do you think they were more guilty than everyone else who lived in Jerusalem? By no means! But I tell you, if you do not repent, you will all perish as they did!" (Luke 13:4-5 [NABRE]).

What Evil Really Is: A Lack of a Due Good

Now to answer the question directly of whether God created evil, the answer is "no." In fact, evil is not something created at all. For St. Thomas, evil is a lack of a due good (ST I, 48, 3). God created all things, and all things he created are good. But bits and pieces of the goodness that belongs to many created things were chipped away by both fault and punishment. Also the order God gave creatures has in many cases been reduced to disorder.

Now simply to lack a certain goodness is not evil. For example, it is not evil that some people are not excellent runners because not everyone needs to be. But it is a physical evil that some people do not have legs because people are meant to have two legs. Furthermore, it is a moral evil (the evil of fault) if someone planted a bomb on a sidewalk which resulted in the person not having those legs. If there were no goodness, there would be no evil. Evil only exists as a parasite to goodness (ST I, 48, 2). For example, if there were no people, there would be no evil of lacking legs. For this reason, there is really no such thing as pure evil (ST I, 48, 4). Even for the Devil, insofar as he is a creature of God, it is a good that he exists. But the beauty and glory that God had given him as an angel of light are very much corrupted by both fault and punishment.

Why God Permits Evil

God permits evil because it is a consequence of the undeniable good of freedom. But then God uses the unfortunate effects of freedom badly used to bring about even greater, higher good. We may never fully understand how until he shows us in Heaven. It is in the mystery of Jesus' death and resurrection that we come to realize the true meaning of suffering and evil. Further, in the end, God will bring about justice for all, rewarding the righteous and punishing the unrighteous – a justice that does not always come about on earth. We know that goodness is infinitely more powerful than evil and that the trials of the present are "as nothing compared to the glory to be revealed for us" (Romans 8:18 [NABRE]). Please see Question 6: "How Does God Rule Creation?" for a further basic explanation of why God permits evil and how he brings good out of it.

Reflection for the Catechist

- o According to Christianity, what is the ultimate diagnosis for the problems of the world? What is the ultimate answer to those problems?
- o What is the ultimate source of the evils we experience today? (See the second paragraph.) How does the distinction of fault and punishment play into that?
- o What is St. Thomas' definition of evil? (See the section "What Evil Really Is.") What is the importance of the word "due" in that definition?
- o How does St. Thomas' understanding of evil yield to an understanding of God being ever present and always in control?
- o Consider two things that are evil: a person dying by murder and a person dying in an earthquake. Are these things evil in the same way? What's the difference?
- o Recall the instances of senseless evil from the first paragraph. Are such things compatible with the existence of an all-good and all-powerful God? If so, how?

Presentation Ideas

Key Concept: God did not create evil. Evil is simply the absence of the goodness God intended for something he created. Evil came into the world because of the sin of our first parents, Adam and Eve.

Question 7: If God Created Everything, Did God Create Evil?

Scripture: "God looked at everything he had made. And he saw that everything was very good."
– Genesis 1:31 (ERV)

Original Sin: How Evil Came into the World

Activity: Ask the students to imagine a world in which:

- We would always be close to God and talk with him as a friend.
- We would not have to go to school because God would give us the knowledge of what is most important to know in life.
- Everyone would always look out for everyone else's true good at all times.
- We would always desire what was really good for us and what really would make us happy.
- We would always be healthy and strong and would never die or know the pain of losing someone.

Ask the students: Is this how the world is now?

Explanation: This is what God gave our first parents, Adam and Eve.
- But as a test, God forbade them to eat of the fruit of the tree of knowledge of good and evil. Tempted by the Devil (who had his own fall from grace previously), they rejected God by sin in eating the fruit anyway. They chose to try to find their own way (Genesis 3).

As a consequence: God took away all of these good things from the human race.
- We are all born with "Original Sin," which separates us from God. Now it is harder to live in goodness and there is a lot of evil to face. But God always promised to send us a Redeemer to bring us back to him and to what he intended for us (Genesis 3:15).
- Now we are freed from Original Sin when we are baptized, but we always live with the consequences of it until we arrive in Heaven. Now we have to face up to temptations to sin from the world, the flesh, and the devil.

Evil Is the Lack of a Good God Intended

Activity: Have the students take a good look at the room they are in. Then briefly turn off the lights (ideally so that there is at least still some dim light left). Then have the students take a good look at the same room with the lights out.

Symbols: The room with the lights on represents the world as God created it – all good. The room with the lights turned out represents what God's world looks like when it is chipped away by evil.

Explanation: Evil is the absence of the good God intended. Humans brought evil into the world by freely turning from God.

Evil Is Something Missing That Should Be There

Discussion: Ask the students which of these is evil:
- That not everyone is the fastest runner
- The someone doesn't have legs to run with

Explanation: The reason the second one is evil is because God intended for people to have legs to run with. People are supposed to have legs. But not everybody has to be the fastest runner.

Moral Evil Vs. Physical Evil

Discussion: Ask the students which is worse:
- That a boy broke his arm because he fell by accident
- That a boy broke his arm because another boy intentionally tried to hurt him

Explanation: The second is much worse. It is called "moral evil" or sin, which is also an offense against God who is all good. The first one is "physical evil." Physical evil (such as getting hurt) happens here and there. That it can happen is part of the punishment on the human race for moral evil.

- Still, if something bad happens to someone, it doesn't necessarily mean God is punishing them in particular.

Jesus Brought Victory over Sin and Evil

Activity: Have the students look at a crucifix. Remind them that Jesus is God come among his people. Ask the students if when God himself came he also experienced evil.

Explanation: Jesus too chose to experience great physical evil in order to do battle with sin and evil. On the cross, Jesus, as both fully God and fully human, offered himself perfectly to the Father. By an infinite act of obedience, he made up for our infinite debt to God caused by sin. He has now conquered sin and evil. He brings victory to us as well. But in this life, we must still struggle with it so that we can be proven loyal to him. In Heaven, evil will be no more and we will experience his full victory.

Meditation: Jesus' Victory over Evil

Revelation 5:1-2, 9-12 [ERV], from a vision given to St. John taking place in Heaven

Reader 1:

Then I saw a scroll in the right hand of the one sitting on the throne.... And I saw a powerful angel, who called in a loud voice, "Who is worthy to break the seals and open the scroll?" ...

Reader 2:

And they all sang a new song to [Jesus] the Lamb:
  "You are worthy to take the scroll
      and to open its seals,
  because you were killed,
      and with your blood sacrifice you
      bought people for God
      from every tribe, language, race of people, and nation.
  You made them to be a kingdom and to be priests for our God.
      And they will rule on the earth."

Reader 3:

Then I looked, and I heard the voices of many angels. The angels were around the throne.... There were thousands and thousands of angels – 10,000 times 10,000. The angels said in a loud voice:
  "All power, wealth, wisdom, and strength belong to the Lamb who was killed.
      He is worthy to receive honor, glory, and praise!"

Question 8: What Is Heaven Like?

Background for the Catechist

Heaven is not just a sentimental notion to ease our natural uneasiness with death. It is not about playing harps or eating whipped yogurt on Cloud Nine. It is not a sandy island beach where the surf is just right. It is not some unexplored planet beyond our galaxy. Heaven is what we are made for.

The Resurrection of the Body

We profess in the Apostles' Creed, "I believe in the **resurrection of the body** and life everlasting." This means that Heaven is a place where people move about in their bodies – but it is not a place we can discover by spaceship. It is more likely in another dimension not perceptible to the senses we have now. And our bodies will not be the same as they are now. First, after death, which is the separation of body and soul, we will be out-of-body, but after the Last Judgment and Resurrection, we will receive our glorified bodies like Jesus had after his resurrection. Since we will have bodies, and bodies are meant to be used, we will likely move about using our bodies in fulfilling ways. These glorified bodies will not be subject to the constraints and limitations we are used to and they will express us perfectly. Not only will our bodies be perfectly strong, healthy, and beautiful, but we will not be constrained to being here but not there, and will be able to be truly present where our spirit takes us.

The Communion of Saints

We will also be together with Jesus and all the saints – those of God's faithful we loved on earth and those we have yet to meet. We will see each other and interact. And since we will have the spiritual vision of God (see Question 4: "What Does God Look Like?"), we will truly know and appreciate one another in light of the perfected knowledge and love God will give us in that most amazing spiritual vision of himself. There will be no hurt, jealousy, shame, or awkwardness, but only true and fulfilling friendship with all.

The Fulfillment of All Desire

As St. Augustine wrote, "You have made us for yourself, O Lord, and our hearts are restless until they rest in you." In Question 4: "What Does God Look Like?" we already saw how God's goodness is what draws out all of our desires, even if we don't understand it that way. While one friend may be good as a listener and another for a good time, God is good in all ways because he is the Source of all goodness. If we saw God as he is, we could want nothing else – we would see how everything else we might want is just a shadow of God.

In Heaven, we get to be with God and behold him forever. Heaven is the fulfillment of God's Kingdom – where everything is fully in accord with God's plan and for our true goodness. It is the whole point of his creation. Will we find this desirable? Yes, because first our desires will be purified to desire what they were made for. This happens through suffering either on earth or after death in Purgatory – and we all know that suffering is an inescapable part of our existence on this side of Heaven. Once we have been purified, we will desire what is truly good for us; then God will grant it to us and we will be truly satisfied. For those who have fundamentally rejected God's love through unrepentant mortal sin, the vision of God would not be a pleasant but rather a terrible thing; hence the alternative to Heaven is Hell, which involves isolation from God and neighbor.

What We Will Do in Heaven

In Heaven, we will never run out of wonderful things to do. Together with the saints, we will go exploring every bend we can of God's endless goodness, truth, and beauty, making full use of our minds, wills, and bodies. With our Spirit, we will see God directly, and with our physical eyes, we will see Jesus, the saints, and the beauties of our heavenly surroundings. Together with the angels, we will join forever in harmonious and heartfelt praise of God.

Reflection for the Catechist

o How will our bodies be different in Heaven than they are now?

o Why will Heaven be appealing in such an ultimate way for all people who arrive there?

o Does Heaven appeal to us, personally, now? Why or why not? What does that tell us about our own values?

o What difference does it make for us in our lives knowing that God destined us for Heaven with our bodies as well?

o If Heaven involves a communion of saints, what does that tell us about our own tendencies to individualism?

Presentation Ideas

Key Concept: Heaven is the place beyond our world where we will be with God forever. In Heaven, we will also walk in perfect harmony with everyone else who loves God. All of our good spiritual, emotional, and physical desires will be completely fulfilled. We will ultimately have "glorified" bodies. These bodies will be perfectly strong, healthy, and beautiful. They will not have the limits that we are used to here on earth. With our renewed bodies and minds, we will go exploring the wonders of God together with the saints. We will never be bored or unhappy in any way.

Scripture: "Better one day in your courts than a thousand elsewhere." – Psalm 84:11 (NABRE)

In Heaven, We Will Be with God and the Saints Forever

Discussion #1: Ask the students: Have you ever been part of a group where everyone was joined together in a single purpose? Or have you ever been in a group where everyone was completely accepting of everyone else? What was it? (Perhaps family, a sports team, a Scout patrol, a group of friends.) What was it like, or would it be like, being part of that kind of group?

Symbolism: A group completely united in purpose and fully accepting of each other represents the relationship of God and the saints in Heaven.

Explanation: We always want to fit in. It's a need that we have, but it's not always met here on earth. We won't have to worry about that at all in Heaven. God knows us and loves us even more than we love ourselves. And the saints are the greatest and most accepting company you could imagine.

Discussion #2: Ask the students to name someone who they know or love who has died.

Tell the students that "saint" means "holy." Not every saint in Heaven is an official canonized saint (raised as an example of heroic holiness for all by the Church). Still, everyone in Heaven is a saint. That means that your loved ones who have died might also be saints, or might be becoming saints.

Explanation: In Heaven, we will be with people who we know and love. We will also come to know and love those we have not yet met.

All Our Good Desires Will Be Completely Fulfilled in Heaven

Discussion #1: Ask the students to name several of the good things that they want.

Explain to the students: Our desires in Heaven will be transformed and will be completely met. Some of our current desires will be "obsolete" in Heaven.

Example #1: Earth is like a very buggy "beta version" of a smart phone app. When the perfected version comes out, no one wants to go back to the beta version. Heaven is the completely amazing experience that everyone wants deep down, even if they don't realize it.

Example #2: Back in the 1980's, every young person wanted a portable – but still bulky – cassette tape player to play a handful of songs on the go. In the 2010's, most young people wouldn't even pay a dollar for one of those. Now they can play all the songs they want on their smart phone or iPod®. These devices are much smaller. You can do so much more with them and can store or stream many times more songs on them. In a similar way, no one in Heaven looks back and longs for the things of earth. It doesn't make any sense.

Example #3: A student wants an iPad® or other tablet very badly. Will there be iPads® in Heaven? Probably not. But all the needs within us that an iPad® fills will be completely met.

Let's think: Why do we want iPads®? What needs do we have?

- iPads® let us connect with anyone, anywhere in the world. But in Heaven, we will be instantly connected with everyone we want to be with.
- We can play fun games on an iPad®. But we won't need to make up anything fun to do in Heaven. We will always be so excited and focusing all our energies on wonderful things – and not just things on a screen.
- iPads® help us find information that we otherwise wouldn't know. But in Heaven, God himself will give us all the knowledge we could ever want.
- iPads® are interesting interesting because they are made up of a lot of advanced technology. But in Heaven, we will explore the depths of God. He is the Creator of the human mind that developed that technology. God can do more than any technology ever could.
- iPads® are "cool," but Heaven is "out of this world" amazing.

Discussion #2: Have the students name one thing they would like to be able to accomplish that they cannot do right now.

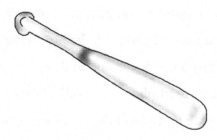

Imagine that a young baseball player wants to get into the big leagues someday. The problem is he is lazy and has no interest in practicing. He only wants to lounge around. Will he ever get there if he stays that way? No.

Some of our desires are more important than others for reaching our goals. The baseball player needs to overcome his desire to lounge around and be lazy so that he can achieve his desire of making it into the big leagues. In the same way, God wants us to desire some things over others.

Ask the students: What are things that God would very much want us to desire? (To serve God and others, to be a good person, to become holy, to help bring about peace and justice in the world, etc.) What are some desires that are less important, if we want to please God? (Getting all the things we want, making lots of money, becoming famous or popular, etc.)

To prepare ourselves for God's free gift of Heaven so that we will truly be able to enter into it and enjoy it, we must value the greater things over the lesser things.

We Will Ultimately Have Glorified Bodies in Heaven

Discussion: Have the students name several things that we cannot do with our bodies that would be helpful. (i.e. Fly, be anywhere at once, be indestructible, be effortlessly strong and beautiful, never get sick or tired, etc.)

Explain to the students: As we say every Sunday at Mass, we "believe in the resurrection of the dead." This means that after the resurrection of the dead at the end of time, we will have our bodies back in Heaven. At that time, God will make them better than they ever were on earth.

In Heaven, our bodies will be indestructible, strong and beautiful, always healthy, and always energized. They will be also able to go instantly anywhere we want to be.

Our bodies are important. They are destined for Heaven and are meant to serve God and others. We must treat our bodies and those of others with respect.

We Will Explore God's Endless Wonders in Heaven

Ask the students: When was the last time you went exploring? What did you explore? What is fun about exploring?

> Symbolism: Exploring represents how we will come to know God's infinite goodness, truth, and beauty for all eternity. We will do this in body and soul and together with the saints. We will never get bored. Instead, we will find out more and more. Everything we experience will be filled with the light of the knowledge of what we discover.

> See activities from Question 4: "What Does God Look Like?"

Review

Ask the students what they are looking forward to the most about Heaven.

Meditation: The House of the Lord

Psalm 84:1-5, 10-12 (ERV)

Reader 1:

LORD All-Powerful, the place where you live is so beautiful!

Lord, I cannot wait to enter your Temple!

    I am so excited!

Every part of me cries out to be with the Living God.

LORD All-Powerful, my King, my God, even the birds have found a home in your Temple.

They make their nests near your altar, and there they have their babies.

Reader 2:

Great blessings belong to those who live at your Temple!

    They continue to praise you.

Great blessings belong to those who depend on you for strength!

    Their heart's desire is to make the trip to your Temple.

One day in your Temple is better than a thousand days anywhere else.

Serving as a guard at the gate of my God's house is better than living in the homes of the wicked.

Reader 3:

The Lord God is our protector and glorious king.

    He blesses us with kindness and honor.

The LORD freely gives every good thing to those who do what is right.

LORD All-Powerful, great blessings belong to those who trust in you!

Question 9: Aren't Humans Just Monkeys with Bigger Brains?

Background for the Catechist

The Similarity between Humans and Animals

There has been a push lately to try to associate humans closely with animals, and many young people have been very intrigued by it. Science-themed documentaries follow around a particular species or examine an ecosystem, and narrators strike chords of empathy within us for the animals. Many of the animals seem just like us – they have feelings such as pain, pleasure, love, anger, and fear. They need to belong to a group and to communicate with it. They show amazing abilities to hunt, make homes for themselves, raise their offspring, and do what they need to survive. We hear about how the dolphin is the "smartest" of the animals. Meanwhile more and more scientists and psychologists are reducing all human behaviors to what is common to the animals. It is said that humans and animals are simply at different stages and branches of the process of evolution. People are glad to hear about this closeness to animals because they love their pets and experience their pets' affection in return – and perhaps because it absolves them from real moral responsibility. And many teachers love to draw out the similarity between animals and humans for students.

A Difference in Kind

Many students think of humans as simply monkeys with more highly evolved brains. Philosophers call this a "difference of degree." In other words, the difference between humans and animals would be that humans have *more* of something – in this case more brain cells and everything that comes with having more brain cells. Certainly, in the realm of biology, a difference of degree does exist between animals and humans. Christians, however, believe that the difference between humans and animals also involves a difference of kind. There is something about humans that evolution by itself could never bring about in a billion years – no pun intended!

St. Thomas Aquinas, writing in the Middle Ages, had great insight into the many things that humans share with animals. He followed Aristotle, who was a great scientist in addition to being a great philosopher. For St. Thomas, an animal is a bodily being that has senses, feelings, motion, and even cognition. At the same time, he realized that despite all the similarities between humans and animals, there is one essential difference that changes the whole game: God created humans with an immaterial spiritual soul.

Humanity: The Rational Animal

St. Thomas defined humanity as a "rational animal." What sets humans apart from all other animals is rationality. **Rationality** involves having the spiritual powers of knowing and willing. These powers color the whole of the human being, raising even many of the aspects he shares with animals to a whole new level. For example, not only can we recognize a tree but we can understand the concept of being a tree and study it. Not only can we know something or feel something, but we know that we know it and know that we feel it. Not only can we choose something, but we choose it for a self-determining purpose and be held morally accountable for that choice – we have free will. Not only do we have feelings of anger, but our anger becomes a moral area to be mastered. Not only do we feel pain, but we can discern meaning in our suffering. Not only can we be part of a group, but we can truly desire the best for others. Not only can we experience creation, but we can trace it back to its Creator and offer him worship.

The Spiritual Soul

The powers of rationality arise from our **spiritual soul** – which is how we are created in the "image of God" (Genesis 1:27). As the life principle of humans, it differs in kind from the life principle of animals, which are purely material. Unlike brain cells and various parts of the nervous system, the spiritual soul is not made of matter. It cannot be directly observed, measured, or weighed. Nor is it a part of the body which can be isolated and mapped out on a chart. It is the principle of life that gives us our human identity. It is created directly by God at the moment of conception in our mother's womb, and its scope reaches towards eternity. Just as it cannot be weighed or measured, neither can it be destroyed because it has no parts to be broken up or changed into something else. So it is destined to live on forever. It is not the body, but it is joined subtly and harmoniously with the body, but it does not cease when it separates from the body in death. Body parts serve it and inform it, but it can do what no body part could ever do – reflect on itself, understand concepts with light from God, and make decisions for self-determining goals.

Imagine even the best of dogs thinking to itself, "I resolve that from now on, I am going to be a truly great dog." It's ridiculous. Such a thing requires spiritual power that dogs do not have. For this reason, God gave humans dominion over and responsibility for all the rest of creation (Genesis 1:28).

Sacramentality: God Reaches the Soul through the Body

For humans in this life, the body mediates the outside world to the soul and the body in turn expresses the soul. The soul is spiritual like God who is Spirit. We come to know the things of God symbolically through things we perceive with our senses. For example, the **sacraments** all have visible signs that express and effect spiritual realities. In Baptism, water poured over the body expresses and effects the cleansing of the soul. Because God is Spirit, he cannot be seen by humans (except through the spiritual vision he gives them in Heaven). But God the Son became human in Jesus. Now the face of Jesus expresses for us the face of God. Now the words and actions of Jesus express the will of God. God reaches our souls through our bodies, as it were, sacramentally.

A Word on Evolution

Some Catholics believe in evolution, others do not. The literary style of the Creation stories in Genesis can be taken as symbolic, given that they express the deeper truths about God, humanity, and creation. Pope John Paul II affirmed that evolution can be consistent with the Catholic faith, given that one's understanding of it does not conflict with what is taught as revealed by God. Pope Pius XII in *Humani Generis* taught that the evolution of the human body can be consistent with the Catholic faith provided that one believes that God directly created the human spiritual soul and that all humanity is historically descendent from Adam and Eve, who faith tells us passed on Original Sin to us. In fact, we believe that *every* human spiritual soul is created directly by God since it cannot possibly arise from matter in mere reproduction. That is why we speak of new human life in terms of "procreation."

Reflection for the Catechist

- o How are humans similar to animals? How are they different?

- o Is the spiritual soul in humans a difference of degree or a difference of kind from the life principle in animals?

- o What is rationality? How does rationality color even much of what humans share with animals?

- o In what ways does God reach us through our bodies?

- o What difference does it make that humans have a spiritual soul – especially with regard to God?

- o Why can't evolution be responsible for the human spiritual soul, even if it may be responsible for the body?

Presentation Ideas

Key concept: Humans are similar to animals in many ways, but one thing makes all the difference. Humans have a spiritual soul and animals do not. The spiritual soul is not made up of parts, so it can never be destroyed. It is also destined to live on forever. Because of our soul, we understand truth, make decisions about ourselves, and have a relationship with God.

Scripture: "God blessed them and God said to them: Be fertile and multiply; fill the earth and subdue it. Have dominion over the fish of the sea, the birds of the air, and all the living things that crawl on the earth." – Genesis 1:28 (NABRE)

Humans Have a Key Difference from Other Animals

Free Will

Discussion: Ask the students if they have any pets. Ask them if their pets can make choices. If you put two bones in front of a dog, the dog will choose the one it finds more interesting.

Have the students consider this: Is it likely that that dog has ever determined to itself to be the best dog that it can be – to be a truly great dog? Of course not.

Explain: Only people can freely make decisions about themselves like that. People can know and understand their goals and choose them freely. That's why only people are responsible for their choices. If a dog is punished for making a mess, that's only so that the dog will associate making a mess with a negative consequence. It's not because the dog has done something morally wrong. Dogs do not have free will. Only people do.

Knowledge

Discussion: Ask the students if animals can think. Animals do have brains and they use them to associate what they see, touch, hear, smell, or feel with certain actions. The dog sees a bone and associates it with eating.

Have the students consider this: Do you think that your dog has ever taken up a study of bones to find out what parts of animals they come from or what types of elements they contain? Or do they write poetry about different types of bones? Or do you think your dog has ever pondered the meaning of life? Of course not.

Explain: Animals do not really understand the things that come into their brains. People, on the other hand, are able to understand things, think about them, study them, or even write poetry about them.

Physical and Spiritual

Write this chart on the blackboard and have the students help fill it out:

	PHYSICAL				SPIRITUAL	
	Material Parts	Life	Senses	Motion	Knowledge and Free Will	Capacity for Relationship with God
Animals	✓	✓	✓	✓		
Humans	✓	✓	✓	✓	✓	✓

Explain: Humans have a life principle that is entirely different from what animals have. Humans have a spiritual soul. This enables us to have rational knowledge, free will, and the possibility for a relationship with God.

The Spiritual Soul

Tell the students: The brain is not the same as the spiritual soul. The spiritual soul uses the brain. But the spiritual soul will continue to think, will, and experience things even after the body has died – and the brain along with it.

Have the students consider: Anything that is made up of parts can be destroyed. How could a pencil get destroyed? It could be broken. It could get used up. It could get ground up or burned. But the spiritual soul is not made up of parts. So it can never get destroyed. It is destined to live forever.

Further: You can't see it, but when you say "I," you meet it. We meet it in the inner self. Then we realize that everything else we do is colored by our spiritual soul.

Question 9: Aren't Humans Just Monkeys with Bigger Brains?

Created in the Image of God

Tell the students: Humans are the only creatures on earth that God created in his own image. Being made in the image of God doesn't mean that we physically look like God. It means that we are created with a spiritual soul and its powers of knowledge and free will.

Further: What difference does it make that we are created in the image of God? It means that we are created with the possibility for having a relationship with God. That makes all the difference.

Evolution and the Difference in Kind

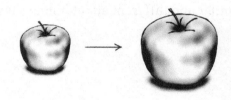
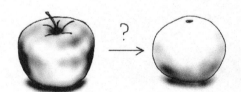

Activity: Bring in an orange and two apples – one bigger and one smaller. While the smaller apple might have become larger if it had been given more time on the tree, it would never have become an orange. As the saying goes, apples are apples and oranges are oranges. (We're not talking about evolution here but just fruit on a tree.) The two apples have a difference in degree. The apple and the orange have a difference in kind.

Explain: The key difference in humans – the spiritual soul – is not a product of evolution. It's like an orange growing on an apple tree. The only way it could have been put there is to be grafted on by someone who got it from an orange tree.

Further: God directly created the spiritual soul of the first human. This is so even if he might have created their body through the process of evolution. In fact, God directly created every human spiritual soul that ever comes to be. Spirit only comes from spirit.

God Often Works in the World through Creatures

Activity #1: How does God usually give us knowledge? Most of the time, God does not directly give us knowledge (though he could). Instead, he works through books, teachers, and experience. Yet in the end, all knowledge comes from God.

Explanation: While God can always work directly in creation, he usually works through creatures. In a similar way, it is possible that God used the process of evolution to bring the physical world to the way it is now after first creating matter from nothing.

Activity #2: Create a chain of causes for familiar things back to God. An example can be found in the activity for the 2nd Way for God's existence "The Coming-To-Be of Things" in Question 1: "Does God Really Exist?"

Review

Have the students explain to each other in small groups what is similar and different about humans and animals.

Meditation: The Role of Humans in God's Creation

Psalm 8:1, 3-9 (ERV)

Reader 1:

LORD our Lord, your name is the most wonderful in all the earth!

I look at the heavens you made with your hands.

     I see the moon and the stars you created.

And I wonder, "Why are people so important to you?

     Why do you even think about them?

Why do you care so much about humans?

     Why do you even notice them?"

Reader 2:

But you made them almost like gods

     and crowned them with glory and honor.

You put them in charge of everything you made.

     You put everything under their control.

People rule over the sheep and cattle and all the wild animals.

They rule over the birds in the sky

     and the fish that swim in the sea.

LORD our Lord, your name is the most wonderful name in all the earth!

Michael J. Ruszala

Question 10: Did Jesus Create the World?

Background for the Catechist

The simple answer to the question is: Yes, but not as human. As romantic as it may sound, it really wasn't the hands of the Baby Jesus who fashioned the world. But the Person of Jesus, who at one point was a baby in his mother's arms, was indeed the Creator of the world along with the Father and the Holy Spirit. A little confusing but also quite fascinating, this student's question touches on two concepts that were very important for St. Thomas. The first is the "**Incarnation**," which means that in Jesus God became human. The second is the "**communication of idioms**" which means that when it comes to Jesus, we can attribute both his divine actions and human actions to him as a person. But first let's review what we mean by "God."

God: Nature and Persons

We might review some of the attributes of God – that he is simple (not made of parts), all perfect and good, infinite, omnipresent (present everywhere), immutable (unable to be changed), eternal (without beginning or end), **omniscient** (all-knowing), and **omnipotent** (all-powerful). All these attributes belong to the "divine nature." He is also the supreme Unity, which is why we rightly refer to God in the singular (i.e. "he") and never the plural. Only Persons are plural in God.

Jesus revealed to us, though, that God is a Trinity – Father, Son, and Holy Spirit. He speaks to us of the Father and prays to him constantly, he tells us that he is one with the Father, and he tells us that he will pray to the Father to send us the Holy Spirit. The Fathers of the Church tell us that the three Persons – Father, Son, and Holy Spirit – share everything of the divine nature (all the attributes of God) in common. The only thing they don't share is their own unique identity, which arises from their relation to each other. The Father is the Origin, the Son is his Word or Image, and the Holy Spirit is the Love that proceeds from them both. Still none came before either of the other Persons – recall that it is part of the divine nature to be eternal.

Jesus is the human name of the Son of God. The Son of God, or Word of God, is equal to the Father and the Holy Spirit, but is not the Father or the Holy Spirit. So it's not true that the Father became human or that the Holy Spirit became human. Only the Son became human, sent by the Father, so that he might communicate to us the Holy Spirit. Yet because the Son became human, we can truly say that God became human.

The Incarnation

"Incarnation" means "becoming flesh." We read of Jesus in John 1:14, "And the Word became flesh and made his dwelling among us" (NABRE). God the Son, who existed from all eternity, joined himself inseparably and forever to human flesh, becoming fully human in time while always being fully God in eternity. He did this to bring salvation to the human race in the most fitting way (ST III, 1, 2). Since God is infinite, St. Thomas says that human sin against God "has a kind of infinity from the infinity of the Divine majesty" (ST III, 1, 2, ad. 2). Humans must make up for their sin, yet because their nature is both finite and fallen, they cannot. But if God himself became human, humanity would be able to offer God perfect satisfaction for sin – and that is precisely what he did. We in turn, can join our own sufferings and good works to his suffering. In becoming human, God also communicated and revealed himself to humanity in the most fitting way – that God might be made visible to humankind through the words and deeds of Jesus. In this way, the spiritual is revealed through the sensible.

The Communication of Idioms: What We Can Say of Jesus

The Person of the Son of God inseparably joins together divine nature and human nature. Natures are the sources of what a being is able to do. For example, humans have the natural power to walk, talk, think, feel, and so forth. Birds of prey have the natural power to fly, grasp, and see at great distances. God, by the divine nature, possesses all the divine attributes discussed above and is able to do all things that are possible – including create the universe from nothing. Because of what is called the "communication of idioms" (a principle used by St. Thomas and others) any action of Jesus, whether it comes from the divine nature or the human nature, is rightly attributed to the Person of Jesus, the Son of God. So, by his human nature, Jesus experienced emotions, as when he wept for Lazarus who had died. And by the divine nature, Jesus created the world and continued holding it in existence, even as he was rocked in his mother's arms as a baby. And yes, he is the only child who was able to pick his own mother beforehand.

Reflection for the Catechist

- o Why did God become human? (See section entitled "The Incarnation.")
- o If God became human, is it right to say that God the Holy Spirit became human? (See the last paragraph of the subsection entitled "God: Nature and Persons." The answer, by the way, is "no.")
- o Why is it that we can say Jesus created the universe but that it was not done by the hands of the Baby Jesus? (See the subsection entitled "The Communication of Idioms: What We Can Say of Jesus.")
- o Why does St. Thomas believe that God becoming human was the most fitting way to redeem the human race? (See the subsection entitled "The Incarnation.")
- o What difference do you think it makes for us as humans that God became human?

Presentation Ideas

Key concept: God the Son became fully human in Jesus while always being fully God. He did this to bring humans back to a right relationship with God. We could not make up for sin on our own. Whenever we talk about Jesus, we're talking about a Person who is both fully God and fully human. So we can say that as human, Jesus felt sad sometimes, and as God, he created the world.

Scripture: "He is the image of the invisible God, the firstborn of all creation. For in him were created all things in Heaven and on earth... all things were created through him and for him. He is before all things, and in him all things hold together." – Colossians 1:15-17 (NABRE)

First: Review What We Know About God

Discussion: Ask the students to name some of the things that God is or can do. Answers may include: know everything, create the world, rule creation, be all-powerful and all-good, etc. Reassert that God can do all these things as God.

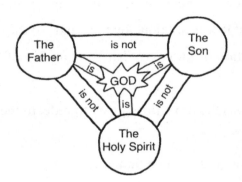

Further: Remind the students that we believe that there are three Persons in one God. Ask them to name the three Persons of the Trinity: Father, Son, and Holy Spirit. They share everything in God. All together they create the world and rule creation, etc. The only thing they don't share is their own identity as distinct Persons.

Explain: But the Persons of the Trinity are distinct from each other. The Father is not the Son and the Son is not the Holy Spirit. Draw a chart on the blackboard like the illustration above to make this point with the students. Quiz them on it.

Why God Became Human

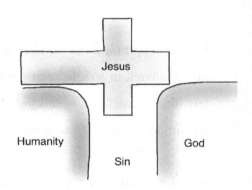

Discussion #1: Explain to the students that sin created a gap between humans and God that was larger than any mere human could fill or make up for. Because of God's infinite greatness, even small sins are very serious because they offend God. Draw an illustration on the blackboard like the one to the side and explain it to the students.

Explain: God the Son became fully human forever in Jesus while always being fully God. So Jesus is fully God and fully human.

Ask the students to share if they know what percentage they are of one nationality or another (only if they want to share). One might be 75% Irish and 25% Italian, for example. But with Jesus, he is 100% God and 100% human.

As God, Jesus did all the things God can do. As human, Jesus did all the things that humans can do. Because he was fully God and fully human, he was able to make up perfectly for the sins of humanity. Ask the students how he did that. It was by the perfect obedience to the Father that he offered through dying on the cross and then rising.

Discussion #2: Ask the students to name a few facts about a friend of theirs. Perhaps he is tall, has brown hair, and plays basketball. Ask the students how they know those things. Probably because they have seen and observed their friend many times.

Explain: God is not visible since he is Spirit. But God made himself visible through Jesus. Now in Jesus and his words and actions, we can see God in the best way possible on earth.

For example: Through the example of Jesus the God-Man, we can know how we should live. Ask the students to name some things we should take as an example from Jesus.

Further: In fact, images of Jesus in our churches follow the example of God who became human. While the ancient Israelites were forbidden to make "graven images," now we can rightly make representations of God in Jesus.

What We Can Say about Jesus

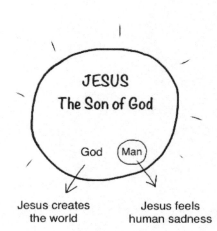

Jesus creates the world   Jesus feels human sadness

Activity: Draw the pictured illustration on the blackboard and explain it.

Explain: Jesus is fully God and fully human. The illustration shows that he is both. We can attribute both his human actions and divine actions to the Person of Jesus, the Son of God.

Ask the students to name some things that Jesus does as God and some things that he does as human. Perhaps write them on the blackboard under the examples already given.

Review for the Students: Have the students answer to each other in small groups whether Jesus created the world. Have them explain their answer.

Meditation: Jesus' Example as God-Man

Philippians 2:5-11 (ERV)

Reader 1:

In your life together, think the way Christ Jesus thought.
He was like God in every way,
   but he did not think that his being equal with God was something to use for his own
benefit.

Reader 2:

Instead, he gave up everything, even his place with God.
   He accepted the role of a servant, appearing in human form.
During his life as a man, he humbled himself by being fully obedient to God,
   even when that caused his death – death on a cross.

Reader 3:

So God raised him up to the most important place
   and gave him the name that is greater than any other name.
God did this so that every person will bow down to honor the name of Jesus.
   Everyone in heaven, on earth, and under the earth will bow.
They will all confess, "Jesus Christ is Lord," and this will bring glory to God the Father.

Michael J. Ruszala

Question 11: If Something Is Wrong in one Culture, Could It Be Right in Another Culture?

Background for the Catechist

Cultural Relativism

During a parish faith formation class on Christian moral teaching, a 7th grade student spoke up confidently that we shouldn't presume that just because something is wrong in our culture it couldn't be right in another culture. Other students agreed. I asked them why they thought that. They said that many of them had a teacher at their public school who teaches that. He says it's wrong for us to judge other cultures. This belief is called "**cultural relativism.**"

Granted some things that are appropriate in certain cultures may be considered rude in other cultures. And it would be morally wrong to be intentionally rude or callous. For example, in Jesus' day, it was customary for guests to have their servants wash the feet of their guests when they came over for a dinner (Luke 7:44). Not to do so was rude. Today, that would just be considered strange. We live in a different culture in which one's feet are not dirtied as much by the journey. But is morality really nothing but cultural conventions like this?

St. Thomas on Law Grounded in a Divine Legislator

For St. Thomas, to have a common Creator is to have a common Law deeper than any of the particular human laws governing this place or that place. All particular laws ought to concretize that Law for the situations of particular communities. Drawing from ancient Greek philosophy as assimilated into the Christian tradition, he calls that Law the Natural Law. The contents of that Law are reflected in the Ten Commandments but are accessible to all humans regardless of culture or religion. Based on the principle of doing good and avoiding evil, the human mind is capable of discerning that it is right to honor and worship God, to respect parents and country, and to avoid murder, stealing, lying, adultery, and envy. The more subtle implications of the Natural Law, though, are not immediately evident to all because of the limits of our fallen human reason. That is why God's revelation sheds light on the Natural Law in addition to building on it.

For St. Thomas, "Law" is a "dictate of practical reason" from someone who governs (ST I-II, 91, 1). The deepest Law of all is the **Eternal Law.** This is the unchanging plan in the eternal mind of God. Next there is the **Natural Law** which is human reason's participation in God's Eternal Law. God creates humans with the ability to grasp the principles of the Natural Law by that first principle of doing good and avoiding evil. Next there is **Positive Law.** This refers to the particular laws of nations and communities which have been handed down for the common good. These laws ought to never contradict the deeper Natural Law, but should

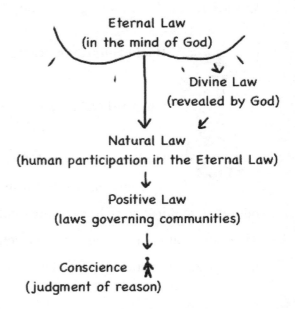

concretize it. For example, laws prohibiting murder reflect the Natural Law in this way. Laws that prohibit drinking and driving reflect the Natural Law in a way that concretizes it for a particular society in which both cars and alcohol exist. But if any positive law violates the Natural Law, then it should be disobeyed in favor of the Natural Law. Unfortunately, nowadays, many positive laws have little connection to the Natural Law, so the connection between the two is not nearly as clear as it was in the days of St. Thomas.

There is still another law for St. Thomas. This law is higher than even the Natural Law but builds on it. It is the **Divine Law**. This is the Law revealed by God in Scripture and Tradition. For example, Jesus taught us to love our enemies and do good to those who persecute us. Such a command is not clear from the Natural Law, and yet it builds on it and reflects the Eternal Law in the mind of God more perfectly.

It should also be noted that **conscience**, for St. Thomas, is the judgment of reason as to what is good and what is bad. Law informs our conscience. With our gift of free will, we have an obligation to follow our conscience, but we are also responsible for forming it well by the laws God has given.

How God Was Taken Out of Morality

This view of morality, with all law grounded in the Divine Legislator, dominated until Immanuel Kant (d. 1804). Kant, a rationalist philosopher but still a religious man, believed that the human mind creates its own laws. But since everyone has the same basic mental structure, the basic laws are the same for everyone. Kant, however, still lived in a time when almost all Europe was Christian, whether Catholic or Protestant, and the basic content of morality was taken for granted. But he removed the Divine Legislator from the picture, and as society moved further away from traditional religion, Kant's theory was taken in more radical directions by other philosophers. Now that there was no Divine Legislator, philosophers tried to find out how to replace him and what to make of morality without God. Was it merely something that came about through natural selection in the process of evolution? Was it something that differed from person to person, or perhaps from culture to culture? Was it simply a statement about how we feel about certain things? Was it a device created by the weak to shame and hold back the strong? Was is entirely relative to the situation? Without God, morality became quite a mess.

Accounting for Errors

God is needed to ground morality. But if Natural Law theory is right that the principles of basic human morality are accessible to all humans regardless of culture or even religion, why are there so many opinions about its content? And why do people often accuse Christians in the public square of appealing to their faith when they say they are appealing to the Natural Law? The reason is that human reason is fallen, thanks to Original Sin passed on from Adam and Eve. Because of that, the fullness of the Natural Law is only discerned by the few, the wise, with great difficulty, and mixed with errors. St. Thomas considered many of the ancient Greek philosophers to be such men. But God's revelation in Scripture and Tradition (through Divine Law) makes the Natural Law known easily, without error, and to all that are open to it. For example, God revealed the Ten Commandments to Moses even though its contents are for the most part already in the Natural Law. But in another example, the Church teaches that based on the prohibitions in the Bible and Tradition against killing and along with what we know from science about fetal development, we can know that abortion is contrary to the Natural Law, even though many people in our society today claim that it is morally acceptable. It should also be noted, though, that in addition to shining light on its contents, the Divine Law also goes beyond the Natural Law in bringing us into God's plan more perfectly.

Cultures Are Judged by God

An implication of Natural Law theory is that God stands above cultures and can judge them. For example, as I explained to the 7th grade students who raised the problem above, the Spartans are an example of a culture which made something culturally acceptable which was in fact morally reprehensible. The rite of passage for a young Spartan warrior involved breaking into the camp of the Helots (their slave class) and killing an innocent person. I explained to the students that the Spartans considered the young warrior who did this to have come of age. They considered it culturally "good." But was it really morally good? The student responded that in their culture it was "good." Other students grimaced in disgust. Then I asked him what God would think of such an act done in Spartan culture. He responded that God would disapprove of it. I asked if God is the Creator of all people or only of the Christians. He responded that he was Creator of all. So the students came to agree that God stands above cultures and can judge cultures as he can judge individuals.

Moral Absolutes

As we saw before, there are many legitimate differences between cultures which reflect the society's orientation to reality. But there is a core that is or at least ought to be the same across cultures, grounded in the Natural Law. This core involves **moral absolutes**. While one culture may require polite hosts to have their guests' feet washed and another culture may not, no culture can rightly sanction the murder of the innocent without being judged by God. The prohibition of the murder of the innocent is a moral absolute that is binding for all peoples of all times and cultures. No situation, however difficult or tear-jerking, could morally warrant the murder of the innocent, even to save many others. It would be morally better to die than to murder the innocent. The Ten Commandments, which gives us the contents of the Natural Law, likewise lists for us the moral absolutes. So ultimately, the Natural Law can never be rightly pushed aside. Circumstances and intentions can make an action better or worse but cannot change the moral character of the act if it goes back to a moral absolute from the Natural Law.

Reflection for the Catechist

o   What may be different in expectations between cultures? What ought to be the same? Why?
o   Why is it so important to acknowledge the Divine Legislator in speaking about morality? And yet how is it that atheists too can practice many of the moral commands?

Question 11: If Something Is Wrong in one Culture, Could It Be Right in Another Culture?

- o How does the Natural Law rely on God while not being tied to any religion? How is it different in this way from Divine Law?

- o What is the connection between God's law and God's plan? In light of this connection, can law be helpful to us or only limiting?

- o What is conscience and how does it help us participate in God's plan?

- o Do you agree that cultures are not beyond judgment when it comes to moral standards?

Presentation Ideas

Key concept: God is the source of all true morality. This is true even for people who are not Christian or who don't believe in God. God stands above both persons and cultures. He can judge them in both justice and mercy by his unchanging standards.

Scripture: "Ever since the creation of the world, his invisible attributes of eternal power and divinity have been able to be understood and perceived in what he has made. As a result, they have no excuse."

– Romans 1:21 (NABRE), on the wrongdoing of the **Gentiles** (non-Jews)

God Stands above Cultures and Persons

Discussion #1: In the ancient Spartan culture, a warrior only came of age after he broke into the camp of the slaves (the Helots) and killed an innocent person. This was approved behavior in the Spartan culture.

Ask the students these questions and discuss their answers:

- o Was that culturally-approved practice morally right?

- o Does God create and rule all peoples or only Christians?

- o What would God think of the practice?

Conclude: God is able to judge both persons and cultures. All morality ultimately comes from God, even if we don't recognize it.

Discussion #2: In Jesus' day, it was expected that a host would have his servants wash the feet of his guests before dinner. This is because people used to wear sandals and the journeys were usually long and dusty.

Ask the students these questions and discuss their answers:
- o Why don't people do that for their guests in our culture?
- o What do people do for their guests when they arrive to come over for dinner nowadays? Perhaps take their coat or hat, offer them a drink.
- o What is common between what is expected of hosts in our day and Jesus' day? What is different and why?

Conclude: Cultures differ from each other. This is because times change, technology changes, the people change, and the way the community expresses itself changes. But common to all cultures is a basic understanding of right and wrong which God gives to all humans.

How God's Plan Comes to Us

Photocopy the graphic organizer below (on a following page) or draw it on the blackboard. Explain it to the students. It shows how God's plan is made known in our lives.

Explain each point:
- o *God's plan* is fully known to him alone but is known to us in our own way by the laws that come from it.
- o The *Natural Law* is the basic standard of right and wrong that God gave all humans.
- o *Civil law* (a form of Positive Law) is the law of our land, which ought to make the Natural Law more real for our community.
- o Our *conscience* is our judgment of right and wrong based on God's laws. We are responsible to God for obeying it and forming it by learning God's laws.
- o *Christ's Law of Love* (the fulfilled form of the Revealed Law) is what Jesus gave to his followers to bring us even closer into God's plan and our own salvation.

Ask the students which concept is being referred to:
- o Stealing is against the law and the police enforce it. (Civil Law or Positive Law)

90

Question 11: If Something Is Wrong in one Culture, Could It Be Right in Another Culture?

o   You know a non-believer who tries to treat everyone with respect. (Natural Law)

o   God's desire for us is to go to Heaven and for us to be happy beyond what we can image. (God's Plan)

o   You know that your grandmother needs help with the dishes, so you take initiative on your own to do them. (Conscience)

o   Jesus said, "Blessed are the poor in spirit, for the kingdom of Heaven in theirs." (Christ's Law of Love or Revealed Law)

Photocopy the second graphic organizer for the students to fill in the blanks from the word bank.

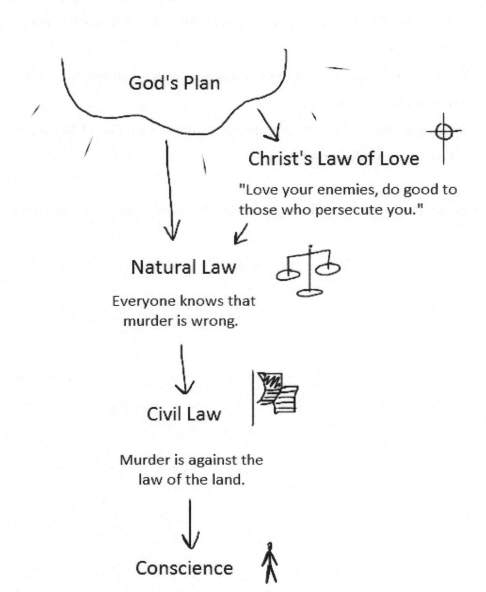

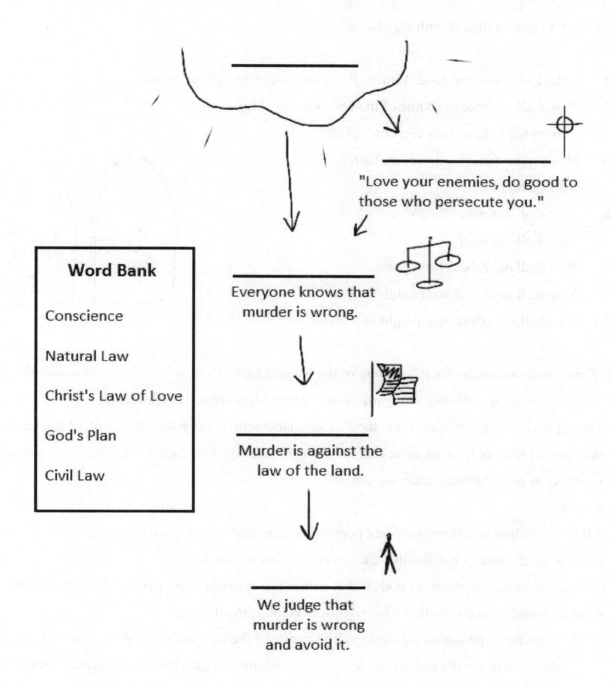

"Love your enemies, do good to those who persecute you."

Word Bank

Conscience

Natural Law

Christ's Law of Love

God's Plan

Civil Law

Everyone knows that murder is wrong.

Murder is against the law of the land.

We judge that murder is wrong and avoid it.

Moral Absolutes

Review the Ten Commandments with the students:

1. I, the Lord, am your God. You shall not have other gods besides me.

2. You shall not take the name of the Lord God in vain.

3. Remember to keep holy the Lord's Day.

4. Honor your father and your mother.

5. You shall not kill.

6. You shall not commit adultery.

7. You shall not steal.

8. You shall not bear false witness.

9. You shall not covet your neighbor's wife.

10. You shall not covet your neighbor's goods.

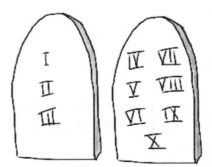

Explain: These commandments are the content of the Natural Law. They are absolute commands that can never be morally put aside. This is true regardless of culture, circumstance, or intention.

o   When speaking of the Natural Law, the 3rd Commandment, to keep holy the Lord's Day, can be taken more universally to set aside time to worship God. Most all cultures in history have done this according to their different understandings.

Ask the students:

o   Is it morally right to kill one innocent person if killing that person would save many others? No. There is an absolute command that can never be morally violated.

o   Is it right to steal somebody's goods if that person is a miser or nasty person? No. There is an absolute prohibition on stealing what rightfully belongs to others.

o   Note that a person dying of starvation may take the necessities he needs to survive because the right to the necessities of life is more fundamental than the right to private property.

Review for the Students

Have the students discuss whether they believe that morality is relative to culture or whether it comes from God who judges all cultures and persons.

Prayer Service: Praise of God's Law

Psalm 19:7-11 (ERV)

Leader: In the Name of the Father, and of the Son, and of the Holy Spirit.

All: Amen.

Side 1: The LORD'S teachings are perfect.
   They give strength to his people.

Side 2: The LORD's rules can be trusted.
   They help even the foolish become wise.

Side 1: The LORD's laws are right.
   They make people happy.

Side 2: The LORD's commands are good.
   They show people the right way to live.

Side 1: Learning respect for the LORD is good.
   It will last forever.

Side 2: The LORD's judgments are right.
   They are completely fair.

Side 1: His teachings are worth more than pure gold.
   They are sweeter than the best honey dripping from the honeycomb.

Side 2: His teachings warn his servants,
   and good things come to those who obey them.

All: Amen.

Michael J. Ruszala

Appendix: The Life and Teachings of St. Thomas Aquinas

18th Century wood carving from the Philippines of St. Thomas Aquinas. Photo by Hiart, in public domain.

Let's take a moment to meet our teacher, St. Thomas Aquinas. St. Thomas Aquinas lived from 1225-1274, born to a noble family of the Kingdom of Naples. Inspired by a Dominican's preaching, he determined at the age of 19 to become a Dominican against his family's wishes. His family imprisoned him in a castle for two years but failed to dissuade him. Afterwards he joined the Dominicans, the Order of Preachers, and was tutored at the University of Paris by St. Albert the Great. St. Thomas is particularly remembered for placing the philosophy of the ancient Greek philosopher Aristotle at the service of Christian theology and for his teaching and example on the unity of faith and human reason.

St. Thomas' most influential works are the *Summa Theologica* and the *Summa Contra Gentiles*, both of which are primary sources for the answers in this guidebook. The *summa* was a popular scholarly style at the time – a systematic summary of theology. The *Summa Theologica*, a very large work that St. Thomas never finished, became a classic for theology students for multiple reasons. In it, St. Thomas summarized the positions of centuries of Church Fathers and theologians, built on a foundation of logic and philosophy from the Greek philosophers through Aristotle, expounded on Scripture and supported his positions with it, presented and demolished countless contemporary and ancient counter opinions, and presented a thorough text explaining the Christian religion from the ground up. Following the scholarly custom of the day, he wrote the *Summa Theologica* in question and answer format. He would ask a question and then present several opinions offering explanations he disagreed with. Next, he would quote Scripture or a Church Father in favor of the position he would present, followed by his own answer to the question. Finally, he responded to the positions that he had previously described, but with which he disagreed. The *Summa Contra Gentiles* is an apologetic work to aide in the explanation and defense of the Christian faith to non-believers. During the Middle Ages, the philosophy of Aristotle first grew in popularity among Islamic scholars before Christian scholars. So in the *Summa Contra Gentiles*, or "Summa Against the Gentiles," St. Thomas explains and defends the Christian faith and understanding of God in Aristotelian terms in dialogue with Islamic and other non-Christian positions.

Glossary

Analogy. A correspondence of two terms such that they are not the same in meaning (univocal), nor completely different (equivocal), but related, such that the term in the purest sense (the prime analogate) governs the likeness of the others. For example, God's Fatherhood is "fatherhood" in its purest sense. Priests represent God's fatherhood in their spiritual care for souls. Human fathers represent God's fatherhood by natural generation and care.

Apologetics. The art of giving a reason for our faith and removing intellectual difficulties and obstacles people have in coming to faith.

Aquinas, St. Thomas (1225-1274). Italian philosopher-theologian, priest of the Dominican Order, and student of St. Albert the Great. Known as the Angelic Doctor, his synthesis of Christian tradition and thorough articulation of doctrine in his *Summa Theologica*, *Summa Contra Gentiles*, and other works has become a perennial benchmark of Catholic scholarship. He is known especially for his appropriation of the philosophy of Aristotle and for his defense of the unity of faith and reason.

Aristotle (384-322 B.C.). Greek philosopher and student of Plato. While Plato placed emphasis on the heavenly causes of the things in the world, Aristotle synthesized Plato's reasoning while emphasizing earthly causes. Through the influence of his teacher St. Albert the Great, St. Thomas Aquinas was among the first medieval Christian scholars to appropriate Aristotle's philosophy to rationally explain and defend the Christian Faith.

Beatific Vision. The supernatural vision of God in Heaven. No creature has the natural power to receive this vision. It must be granted by God. Once granted, it is final because it satisfies all desire and leaves no room for choosing lesser things.

Being. That which is common to all things that exist. The opposite of nothingness. Convertible with goodness, truth, and beauty. A fundamental distinction is made between created and uncreated being.

Beauty. That which pleases the intellect by way of its order and harmony. Convertible with being, truth, and goodness.

Body. A material unity that has parts. Could refer to a living body or an inanimate body.

Catechesis. The process within the Church of handing on the faith. It promotes knowledge of the faith, moral and liturgical formation, formation in prayer, socialization into the life of the community, and ultimately sharing one's faith with others (GDC no. 85-86).

Communication of Idioms. The principle that we can attribute both the divine and human actions of Jesus to him since he is a single person with both sets of powers.

Concupiscence. The human tendency to want more of a good thing than is proper. Though not a sin in itself, if freely acted upon, it leads towards such things as lust, greed, gluttony, and so forth. It comes as a result of the fall of Adam and Eve.

Conscience. A judgment of reason on something as good and therefore to be done or evil and therefore to be avoided. Everyone must obey their conscience, but everyone also has a responsibility to form their conscience in light of God's laws as they are able to know them.

Contingency. Possible to be different than it is. Lacking necessity. Possible not to be. Depends on something else in order to exist.

Cultural Relativism. The belief that morality is ultimately derived from one's culture and hence that morality is relative to culture without any universal moral absolutes.

Devil. Lucifer, an angel created good but who fell from grace by his choice not to serve God.

Divine Law. Law supernaturally revealed by God, such as through the Old or New Covenants.

Essence. What a thing is and what powers or capabilities it has.

Eternal. Having no beginning or end. Only God is eternal is the full sense.

Eternal Law. The plan in the eternal mind of God fully understood by him alone but shown to us through the Divine Law, Natural Law, and human laws which reflect those higher standards.

Evil. The lack of a due good. Evil is divided into fault and punishment, by which fault is rectified.

Evolution. The scientific theory that higher biological forms descended from lower biological forms through natural selection by the survival of the fittest. For Catholics, it is a possible way in which the human body was formed, although it cannot account for the spiritual soul.

Final End. The goal or purpose of a being as created by God. The ultimate final end of all creatures lies in God, though in various ways.

Gentiles. Non-Jews. God's supernatural revelation was not preached to them until the coming of Christ.

Glory of God. That God's infinite goodness and perfection be communicated and made known to all.

Goodness. That which corresponds to our natural, God-given desires. Convertible with being, truth, and beauty.

Heaven. Both a place and a state of being. As a state, it involves the vision of God and the fulfillment of all desire. As a place (beyond this world), it involves physical interaction with the communion of saints after the resurrection of the body.

Human. In past times referred to simply as "man," the reference to "humans" or "humanity" in this book refers to "human nature." Human nature is common to all humans and includes our essential features. For example, it belongs to human nature to have a body and a soul and for the soul to have the powers of mind and free will.

Hypotenuse. The longest side of a right-angled triangle. It can also be formed by drawing a straight line from one corner of a square or rectangle to the opposite corner. Straight lines drawn in this way are always and necessarily longer than the sides of the figure.

Image of God. The rationality of creatures (angels and humans), as seen in the spiritual powers of mind and free will.

Immutability. Attribute of God whereby he is immune to change, including corruption.

Incarnation. The event of the Second Person of the Trinity (the Son or God, Word of God) taking on humanity and being inseparably joined to it such that Jesus is fully God and fully human. The Incarnation makes God present to us through our senses in the most perfect way and makes it possible for humanity to make up for sin through Jesus.

Intellect. Spiritual power to know according to universals (thus abstractly). In humans, it is not to be confused with the brain, but works with it. The intellect is a natural power and thus still exists in humans even if not actualized, such as in the womb. (In this book, "mind" is used synonymously with intellect.)

Intelligibility. The capability for a thing to be potentially understood by a rational mind for what it is and what essential attributes it has.

Law. An ordinance of reason given by a governing authority for the common good.

Love. An act of the will by which one desires for the good of the one loved and for a certain union with them (corresponding to the type of love).

Matter. Anything that has mass and takes up space. It is distinguished from spirit, which really exists but has no mass and does not take up space.

Metaphysics. The philosophy of being. Studies the order of that which is common to all things.

Moral Absolutes. Precepts of the Natural Law that are binding in all times and places regardless of circumstances or intentions. An example is the prohibition against murdering the innocent.

Natural Law. Human participation in God's plan through the Eternal Law. It is binding on all peoples and cultures regardless of religion. Some points may not be clear to all because human reason is fallen. That is why God sheds light on the Natural Law through revelation, as through the Ten Commandments which also reveal its content.

Natural Power. An ability implanted by creation within a given species by which the creature pursues its final end. Intellect and will are examples of natural powers in humans. A natural power is considered a "potency," and when used it is "actualized."

Necessary Being. God: the Being whose essence is his existence, and thus is Being Itself and the Source of all contingent being.

Omnipotence. Attribute of God by which he can do all that it is possible to do. Logically, this follows upon God's goodness, since God has every perfection.

Omnipresence. Attribute of God by which he is present at once to all creation. Logically, it follows upon his infinity.

Omniscience. Attribute of God whereby he knows all things through knowing himself.

Original Sin. The sin all humans (except Jesus and Mary) inherited from Adam and Eve. The consequences of Original Sin are the withholding of God's grace, ignorance of essential truths, tendency to malice of will, disorder of the desires, suffering, and death. The remedy is baptism into Christ and consequently the pursuit of holiness.

Pantheism. Belief in many gods.

Perfection. Completed goodness, actualized power. God has every perfection.

Philosophy. The abstract study of the causes of things by way of natural reason. Literally "the love of wisdom."

Positive Law. Laws established for nations or communities. Positive Law ought to reflect the Natural Law even though this is not always the case. Those cases in which Positive Law contradicts either the Natural Law or Divine Law, it must be disobeyed in favor of the higher law.

Providence. God's foresight for the ordering of all creation. Firstly, it consists in God's ordering creatures by implanting in them their final end. Secondly it consists in God's governance of all events of creation to the greater good.

Resurrection of the Body. The basic Christian belief that at the end of time both the righteous and the unrighteous will receive a resurrected body.

Rationality. The spiritual powers of mind and free will.

Sacrament. A sign instituted by Christ to give grace such that the sign effects what it symbolizes.

Sanctifying Grace. The free gift of God in our souls that makes us pleasing to him and which is required for salvation. A person with sanctifying grace has the dwelling of God in their soul and has the virtues of faith, hope, and charity. Sanctifying grace is distinguished from actual grace, which is a gift of God that moves us in the direction of receiving sanctifying grace.

Secondary Cause. A cause that is intermediate in a chain of events.

Simplicity. Attribute of God whereby he has no parts. Logically, it follows upon God's being Spirit and is the reason for his immutability.

Soul. The life principle of a body. For Aristotle and St. Thomas, animals are said to have material souls, although that language is not found in this book so as to avoid confusion with the human soul which is spiritual.

Spirit. Immaterial being (substance) with mind and free will.

Spiritual Soul. An immaterial soul which is part of what it means to be human. As spiritual, it has the powers of mind and free will. As a soul, it animates the human body as its life principle.

Supernatural. Beyond a creature's natural powers. For example, the Beatific Vision is supernatural to both angels and humans; is a gift from God.

Teleology. Relating to the final end / cause of things.

Theism. Belief in one God.

Transcendence of God. The understanding that God is beyond all creatures such that nothing can be said of God and creatures in the same way (univocally). St. Thomas argues, however, that the same can said of God and creatures by analogy.

Transcendentals. Unity, Being, Goodness, Truth, and Beauty are convertible – or the same in reality – while corresponding differently to our natural powers. Unity corresponds to our intellectual perception of the unity of being. Goodness is being as it appeals to our natural desires. Truth is being as it is understood by our intellect. Beauty is being as it appeals to our intellect by its order and harmony. The transcendentals are experienced in created things, but by analogy reflect God.

Truth. Being as it corresponds to the intellect.

Trinity. The Christian belief that God is one in three Persons. The Father is the Origin, the Son is eternally begotten of the Father, and the Holy Spirit eternally proceeds from the Father and the Son.

Michael J. Ruszala

About the Author

Michael J. Ruszala is a Catholic lay ministry professional. He holds an M.A. in Theology & Christian Ministry and a B.A. in Philosophy and Theology *summa cum laude* from Franciscan University of Steubenville and is certified as a parish catechetical leader by the Diocese of Buffalo. Michael served for over five years as director of lifelong faith formation at a parish in the Diocese of Buffalo, where he started a number of creative catechetical initiatives with children, youth, and adults. He currently works as a parish music director and also serves as an adjunct lecturer in religious studies at Niagara University in Lewiston, NY, where he has taught on Christian Ministry and Popes in the Modern World. He is the author of five religious books including *Pope Francis: Pastor of Mercy*, *David and the Psalms*, and *Saint Padre Pio: In the Footsteps of Saint Francis*.

Michael is an active member of the Society of Catholic Social Scientists, is a former member of two catechetical committees for the Diocese of Buffalo, and is the recipient of the 2016 Christian Service Award from the Canisius College Sodality of Our Lady in Buffalo. He has also been published in religious journals including the *Social Justice Review*, the *Catholic Social Science Review*, and *Lay Witness* online edition. With interests in music, art, tennis, and kayaking, Michael also enjoys directing the children's choir at his parish. Please visit **www.michaeljruszala.com** for more information.

Made in the USA
Monee, IL
10 December 2023